MARTIN FERRIS: MAN OF KERRY
THE AUTHORISED BIOGRAPHY

J.J. BARRETT

MARTIN FERRIS
MAN OF KERRY

BRANDON

First published in 2005 by Brandon
an imprint of Mount Eagle Publications
Dingle, Co. Kerry, Ireland and
Unit 3, Olympia Trading Estate, Coburg Road,
London N22 6TZ, England

2 4 6 8 10 9 7 5 3 1

ISBN 0 86322 310 9

Cover design by id communications, Tralee, Co. Kerry
Typesetting by Red Barn Publishing, Skeagh, Skibbereen
Printed in the UK

CONTENTS

Acknowledgements
Tim Pat Coogan, John O'Mahony, Marie Ferris, Toireasa Ferris MCC, Áine Lynch, Michael Costello, Eamon Browne and Michael Lynch (Kerry County Library), Pádraig Kennelly (*Kerry's Eye*), Skipper Mike Browne, Johnny McCarthy, James Sheehan, Brian Ferris, the inimitable Dan Bally Keating and the late Denis "Denna" Fitzgerald of Rock Street, Tralee.

Dedication

To Marie Ferris and her six children:
Eamon, Cianán, Máirtín, Oonagh, Deirdre and Toireasa
and their grandmother, the late Agnes Ferris

FOREWORD

KERRY IS DIFFERENT – as any Dubliner will tell you! It is said that "Kerry people make the best friends and the worst enemies." Its people seem to have two main directions: onward and upward. This circumstance is said to have come about shortly after the foundation of heaven. Naturally, a Dubliner was one of the first arrivals. He discovered that the good Lord was still working on the original template for a Kerryman. The Dub deliberately distracted the Creator by singing a few bars of "Molly Malone" so that God left out one essential component from the template – the reverse gear!

This forward momentum quality is allied to a talent for scholarship. I once asked a dauntless Kerryman, the late Maynooth Professor Fr Sean Quinlan, if he could explain why it was that Listowel, in particular, seemed to produce such an unending stream of writers and civil servants, and he replied: "'Tis simple, boy! High mountains and good teachers." Geography and scholarship. It was a good answer, but it left out another essential component of the

Kerryman: his history. The history of his country, his county, his county, his sport. These are quite particularist. The geography which decreed that the O'Connells could trade, and be educated, in France also allowed for other aspects of Gaelic individualism to survive. I have met an old man who told me that in his youth he remembered the old four goalposts once used in Gaelic football (and still used in Australian rules) still standing in a sports field near Derrynane.

Other, darker memories, nearer to our time, also linger, though some either deliberately attempt to forget or to cope with the past through that time-honoured Irish coping mechanism – humour.

I remember the famous Church of Ireland clergyman Charles Gray-Stack telling me an anecdote concerning his appointment as Dean of Ardfert. Before taking up the appointment, he attempted to familiarise himself with as many aspects of Kerry's history as he could, and one day he set off for Ballyseedy.

After losing his way, he was told by a local to "Keep straight on until you come to the crossroad and then ask anyone." As similar directions had led to his becoming lost in the first place, Charles asked doubtfully, "But are you sure people will know the way?"

To which the Kerryman replied, "Oh be God they will. Sure the sparks is falling yet . . ."

They were and they are. Not so long ago I was taken on a Homeric tour of the Kingdom by two Kerry friends. The itinerary focussed on vital areas of their formation: great deeds of romantic Kerry, the homes of great GAA footballers, scenery of heart-stopping beauty and the scenes of terrible ambushes and atrocities.

Romance, of course, plays no part in Jo Jo Barrett's chronicle of Martin Ferris's life, but it is out of the other elements of the Kerry matrix – scholarship, high mountains, the GAA and history – that Barrett, Ferris and this valuable book were fashioned.

Both grew up in the shadow of Sliabh Mis. Both sported and played through the parishes of Churchill, Fenit, Barrow and Spa. Both became GAA icons: Jo Jo, the son of another GAA immortal, Joe Barrett, played in four All-Ireland finals; Martin would certainly have done so also had not republicanism intervened. He won an All-Ireland Under-21 medal in 1973. These are no slight men, and the story of how Martin went on to contribute to the story of his county and his country is a compelling one, which nobody is better fitted than Jo Jo to write.

A great poet once wrote of an incident in his formation: "Out of such a local row was *The Iliad* made." Local rows in Ferris's case include illegal salmon fishing, the Fenit oyster war, the saga of the *Marita Ann*, hunger striking in Portlaoise Jail and the debate over the peace process.

I first met Martin in Portlaoise, where I was giving a lecture, as this debate was reaching a crescendo approaching the ceasefire of 1994. An immaculately groomed figure in a light coloured suit, he was courteous and friendly and presented me with two gifts. One was a beautifully worked leather wallet bearing my name and an inscription from the "Portlaoise POWs", and the other a bulky secret history of the jail written by the prisoners themselves.

This was somewhat uncomfortable, as he whispered to me that the warders were looking for the history and I would have to be careful to hide it on the way out. So I left the jail, after an uneasy drink with the governor, with a large subversive document secreted on my person!

A gentler aspect of his life which bore him up while other aspects of his career were bearing him down was the love of his wife Marie. She reared his children without his income, or his presence, while he spent ten years in jail. Very literally a case of "They also serve . . ."

As everyone now knows, Martin emerged from prison and went on to visit Downing Street as a member of a Sinn Féin delegation. More importantly, he became a Sinn Féin TD, ironically winning a seat from the popular Dick

Spring, who had done so much to further the peace process during his period as foreign minister and deputy prime minister.

As this is written, the peace process debate is still raging. Force v. constitutional action. It is the oldest, most gut-wrenching controversy in Irish political life. From it have emerged Cumann na nGaedheal, Fianna Fáil, Clann na Phoblachta, Sinn Féin the Workers' Party and the Democratic Left, which has morphed into the Labour Party and provided it with its present leader.

Martin's son Eamon has followed in his footsteps to a degree, in as much as he too has become a talented footballer. For his sake, and all the other Eamons in Kerry and throughout Ireland, I hope that Martin's side wins out in the peace process debate and that no further chapters need to be written in that Portlaoise history. But whatever happens, I can recommend this story of how at least one quintessential Kerryman came to beat his sword into a ploughshare. It is a tale told in friendship and admiration by the man best qualified to do it, his friend and fellow Man of Kerry, J.J. Barrett.

Tim Pat Coogan

CHAPTER ONE

KNOCKAUNE IS A peninsula rising like a strong shoulder over Barrow Harbour, Barrow beaches, Poll Gorm and Sandy Lane. Scenes for David Lean's epic film, *Ryan's Daughter*, were shot there in 1969. The doomed love story surrounding Robert Mitchum's and Sarah Miles's performances captured the magic of the place. On a good day the sun shines on top of Knockaune hill without hindrance or shadow from dawn to dusk. Fishing was good, and there were few places better in which to grow floury potatoes, carrots and onions, or to hunt the abundant rabbit population. Now the Arnold Palmer designed Tralee Golf Club covers much of the land there.

Agnes and Patie Ferris were living up in Knockaune in Patie's brother Mautie's house when Martin Ferris was born on 28 March 1952 in St Anne's nursing home in Strand Street, Tralee. Immediately next door to the nursing home was the home of Kerry Labour politician and former Kerry footballer Dan Spring, where his son Dick Spring, future Labour Party leader, was reared. About ten doors up from there was the home of IRA Volunteer Charlie Kerins, who was hanged by Eamon de Valera's Fianna Fáil government on 1 December 1944.

The Ferris family lived in Martin's Uncle Mautie's cottage on top of Knockaune hill until Martin was three and a half years of age. Terrible sadness visited the family when Martin's infant sister Mary died shortly after being born in 1955. They then moved down the hill to water's edge to caretake Barrow House for his aunt, Mrs Nelly Griffiths. She was a wealthy emigrant preparing to return to Ireland ten years later. She asked her brother Patie to look after her property for a decade before she finally settled back in Ireland. Barrow House had been a home of the Knight of Kerry, Captain Fitzgerald, and the elderly man retained a holiday flat on the third floor of the elegant old building while Patie, Agnes and family occupied the rest of the beautiful house. It is a wonderful place, especially at high tide, with the sea lapping just feet away from the charmingly designed and situated house. During the War of Independence and the Civil War, the local IRA took over the house as a training camp. It was probably because of its remoteness and usefulness to the local column that it was never burned, as was the fate of so many other houses of the ruling class during the War of Independence. It was the daughter of the Knight of Kerry, Lady Rosanna, who saved young Martin from almost certain drowning after he climbed perilously on the sea wall outside a protective wire barrier, with a full tide just feet below him, in front of Barrow House. From a top window she saw the danger unfolding and raced to the child's rescue.

His younger brother Brian was born on 30 August 1953. From as soon as he could barely toddle, Brian was seldom less than a few paces behind his older brother. They were close then and have always been so down the good and bad days of their turbulent lives. An albino, Brian stood out with his white hair and skin, and he became one of the strongest and hardiest men in the parish. He shared Martin's love of Gaelic football and his political beliefs throughout the Troubles in the Six Counties of the north of Ireland. Brian was possibly arrested even more often than Martin during those years. But for weak eyesight, the younger brother could also have fulfilled the promise he showed as a juvenile footballer. Brian was to run the family farm during Martin's many years of enforced absence from life on the land and is still the farmer in the family.

Barrow has been kind to the Ferris brothers in memories. It is to a great extent scenically privileged, with clean air and general surrounding aspect of the vast sea, beaches and mountains from different viewpoints. The only drawback it held for Martin was isolation from other children, as Brian and he were the only ones of their age on the peninsula when he was very young. When he began school there was only himself and his cousin, Noreen Ferris, going the road from Barrow Peninsula. She was older and in sixth class when he was in high infants. It remained like that until Paddy Bill O'Sullivan's kids, Jimmy Ferris from Ballyea and eventually Brian joined them on the academic road to Barrow National School.

Their father owned a thresher for hire, and the young Martin enjoyed the excitement attached to moving the machine around the locality. To get up Knockaune height, the giant machine needed the assistance of two tractors to pull it up the steep incline.

"I suppose my farthest back memory is of when I was three. I remember my dad having to get the machine up to Paddy Bill's farm. It was an almost impossible task at the time. Or at least I thought so in my young mind. He would thresh corn for Mick Joe Rayel, Paddy Bill, and the Devanes had a bit of corn too. All the people around us had a bit of corn. My dad did the threshing for hire for all of them at the time." No television programme could surpass the joyous recall of being at your father's side as he overcame those seemingly impossible odds.

Donal and Maggie Devane were Martin's earliest and nearest neighbours at the furze-covered Locka on Knockaune hill. They were also his closest neighbours at Barrow House. This much loved couple lived at the bottom of the hill at water's edge, but their land ran up the steep hill to Martin's Uncle Mautie's house, which was Martin's earliest abode. The Devanes always grazed a goat there for her milk. She was locked into a paddock alongside the Ferris cottage. Mrs Ferris would tie the gate and lock Martin into the haggard adjoining the fettered goat's little field. On many occasions there was an SOS out for the three-year-old youngster, who would inevitably be found clinging to the goat's meg.

Martin's childhood risk-taking with the goat brings memories flooding back. "I climbed out of any place they put me, except Portlaoise," he joked.

Big Donal Devane was a smashing man. There is hardly a week in my life that I don't think of him. He is dead now since shortly after I was jailed in 1984. I think he died in 1985. I thought of him a lot when I was in jail. He and I were great friends. He had great yarns, and he was the best man to tell a convincing lie and make you believe the unbelievable. He was also known as Dan Devane. As a child I believed the most astonishing stories from him. He was a big pleasant man and a fabulous character. He was married to my father's cousin, Mag. She was Mag O'Sullivan, and she and my father were always arguing. Donal Devane and Mag O'Sullivan had no kids, but Mag and himself were as happy a couple as you could wish to meet. When we were living near them in Barrow House, they drew water from the well in front of Barrow House every day. Donal would come over every morning for his two buckets of water. Maybe in summertime Mag would come again in the afternoon for another bucket of water. And they would walk the half-mile, fill the bucket of water and walk back again. They had no sanitation in the cottage. They just had electricity, and they lived a very simple, happy life together. It was a beautiful spot altogether in which to live, down at the edge of the tide.

When they were living in Barrow House, Patie Ferris made full use of the marvellous walled garden to produce the tastiest of early potato crops, and onions and carrots too. He supplied the early spuds for the Dublin market. Mrs Swift from Brandon, an Englishwoman with a superior upper-class accent, was first in Kerry to reach the Dublin market each year with early spuds. Patie was usually second. He had to work at it, but he won the annual battle against frost and blight by burning bales of straw around the garden periphery in order to protect the early potatoes from potential disaster. Barrow spuds survived the worst of the famine in the 1840s.

Patie came from a family of seventeen children. They had a cottage and a half-acre on the side of the road alongside where Mautie's cottage was eventually built in Knockaune. Martin heard his father relate that four of his siblings died young, before the age of five years, and two of them died at the age of eight and nine. Eleven survived into adulthood. He left for America in 1925, a route most of his brothers and sisters were eventually to travel. He often spoke about the Black and Tans in the 1921 period. Because Patie was from fifteen to eighteen years old when the two Irish wars – the War of Independence and the Civil War – were at their worst, he had a clear memory of those times. He would recall when the local IRA took over Barrow House as training and living quarters.

The first song Martin can remember his father singing was "Kevin Barry". He would tell the youngster all about how Barry was hanged by the British. The fact that Barry was "just a lad of eighteen summers" made a big impression on the young Ferris. The history of that time was related to young Martin during periods of working together on the farm or when out fishing in their boat.

Patie's politics were basically worker centred. He wasn't a republican. He had a strong sense of justice for the poorer man. Martin remembers that he voted for Tom O'Higgins of Fine Gael in the presidential election of 1966, against Eamon de Valera of Fianna Fáil, because he said O'Higgins had a larger family to keep and wasn't as well off as de Valera. This rationale hardly made sense considering the legal qualifications of O'Higgins, but to Patie Ferris it was as good a reason as any for casting his vote in a "fair" fashion for the underdog.

Patie's work and his family were his life. He had very little education at all before he emigrated to America in 1925 at the age of twenty years. He worked hard in the USA until he returned home again to Barrow in 1945. He saw hard times during the Great Depression in the United States. Then having survived the "Crash" of the twenties and the Depression of the thirties, he laboured hard to survive the harsh post-World War II years of the late forties. However, he earned enough dollars to fund the beginnings of his farming and fishing venture back home in Barrow.

Patie Ferris's other great interest in life was professional boxing. The world boxing monthly publication, *Ring Magazine*, was a regular purchase in the house as he kept up his lifelong love for a sport which he had followed when he was in the USA. A respectable pugilist himself, Patie had in fact boxed in the preliminary rounds of the Golden Gloves Championships when he was a young man. So Martin Ferris was familiar with the names of such sporting heroes as Joe Louis, Rocky Marciano, Jersey Joe Walcott and Sugar Ray Robinson from that golden era of great gladiators in the history of the ring. Martin is still interested in the sport.

Martin's mother, Agnes Mullins, was born in Jamesborough, Limerick, where her father was a train driver. At an early stage her family moved to Ballysimon Road in Limerick city, where she was reared. While visiting her friends the Slatterys of Barrow in 1950 she met Patie

Ferris, who was home after a three-year spell in the USA from 1947 to 1950. As he earned and saved, he would sink money into purchasing his holding back in Ireland. He bought Knockaune with money he made in the USA during his previous period of emigration up to 1945. Romance blossomed and they were married late in the Marian Year.

Martin's mother was Fianna Fáil to the backbone. It is significant that she had a serious dislike for the Free State army. In Limerick, where she had lived, IRA volunteers had been tied by their legs to the army lorries and dragged behind the troop-carrying vehicles to certain agonising death before they reached the barracks with their heads so battered as to be unrecognisable. These horrific incidents left a lasting impression on the young girl.

Agnes was a practising Catholic and, throughout her life, an exceptionally strong believer. Martin remembers the household environment in which he grew up as a very religious one.

> We had the rosary every night, and so we were only young fellows when the religious awareness began to sink in. Then we had to fulfil the First Fridays, as well as every Sunday morning we would have to attend first mass. At first mass we would receive Holy Communion, and so according to the strict rules of the time you were fasting since midnight. My mother always tried to attend first mass. When we were living in Barrow House, she would take Brian and myself with her, and then when we returned my father would set off for last mass. He would have the cows milked and other such chores done around the farm before going up to the church.
>
> I debated a lot about religion with my mother. She would tolerate nothing bad being said against the Catholic religion. I would argue against religion just to get her going, but she was well able to vigorously defend the Catholic Church and religion. My mother was much more intellectual than my father. She was

a great reader of books and newspapers. She watched television and was an avid listener to the radio.

Her faith was unreal throughout her life. It got her through very difficult times in her life. She had a stroke at a young age and lost her hearing and her balance when walking. Still she overcame all of that, and she wore a hearing aid. She suffered terribly when my sister, Mary, died young. My mother also had major surgery, including a hysterectomy, which nearly killed her, but her religious devotion kept her going. She lived with chronic asthma and bronchitis for most of her life.

A cousin of Martin's father named Jim Ferris lived in a cottage west of Donal and Maggie Devane at water's edge too. His "born free" type of lifestyle registered greatly with the young Ferris. Jim's nickname was Kane.

"Jim 'Kane' Ferris was the only man I knew who didn't go to mass in those days. He never went to church. He was a kind of surly individual in ways, but I liked him a lot."

Jim was a powerfully built man with a ruddy, shiny complexion, always in a navy blue polo neck jumper and a cloth cap, and he possessed incredible physical strength in his broad shoulders. He moved heavy boats around the beach with knowing and able ease. Nobody would argue with him. His hands were two or three times the size of a normal man's, and they were misshapen from hard work and well pickled from daily immersion in salt water.

Jim was a first cousin of my father. It was said locally that Jim had time for romance too. There were two eccentric Englishwomen living near by. Jim was caretaker, gardener, boatman and general handyman for the two women. These women were also the first gay couple we ever heard tell of. They actually lived openly as a couple in the parish. Although at the time we knew very little about these things. Jim would give the impression that he was much friendlier with one of the two women than people thought. But that is another story. Jim Kane reckoned anyway that they were both in love with him and that he was looking after them.

Martin went fishing with the older man quite a lot when he was a young fellow. Jim had a good boat and was a fine boatman. He also had a trammel net and a hauling net in which he got all kinds of edible fish. He got pollock, mackerel and sea bass, turbot, brill, plaice and the odd few salmon in summertime. Martin's uncle, Jack Ferris, a brother of his father Patie, and who was known as Jackdaw, would go with them quite often to set a spiller if fishing was good. Though an illegal means of fishing, they could catch good quality fish too, like turbot and brill. From these hardened and knowledgeable men, Martin knew every bit of the channels in Barrow Harbour. Between Jim and his father, he learned about every hazard, rock and ripple. Jim was the best man he ever met for harvesting the sea and also, strangely enough, for relaying ridiculous riddles. When they would be out in the boat, patiently waiting for the nets or lines to fill, they would be sitting back in the floor of the boat listening to the water lapping or just easily rolling with a gentle swell. Martin recounts:

> That was when Jim would start off with his riddles and rhymes. He lived a very simple and pleasant life. He really lived off nature, because he grew his own potatoes and cabbage and all the necessary things that kept him going throughout the seasons. He had fish for no cost, except his time, and he would kill a pig for the bacon and have it hanging up curing inside in the kitchen. I learned about the tides and winds and weather, and mostly all from Jim Kane Ferris. Fishing under the shadow of historic Barrow Castle at dawn on a summer morning as the sun comes up was as near as one could get to heaven. This we did many times in Jim's boat, and in my father's boat too.

21

And when the sun heated the rocks and warmed the water at high tide, Martin thought it was the best place in the world in which to swim. Jim told him all about the right baits and when to go for silver eels, for worms, and then where to fish with them. He explained that the best time to go fishing in Barrow Harbour is at the turn of the tide. He made out that when the tide turns the fish are feeding and that is the best time to go.

Like his cousin Jim Kane, Martin's uncle Jack was an expert rabbit snarer, and he also taught his nephew everything he knew about hunting. By the age of ten Martin was reasonably adept at finding his way around nature's plentiful bounties in Barrow.

The taming of Martin Ferris's young wildness was a task first undertaken by the female teachers at Barrow National School.

"I hated school, period. I just loved the open countryside and the sea," says Martin.

But he admits that the only school he was ever reasonably happy in was Barrow National School.

That's the only school I ever liked. I was happy and enjoyed going there. After that I hated all schools right across the board. Hated every day I had to attend school. Although I felt caged in no matter what school I attended, I tolerated Barrow School. There was something about its size and its cut sandstone walls that made it feel comfortable. It was situated close to the fields too. Corn and other crops were growing just a few feet away. I suppose it was so small, and the teachers were very nice too, that it was where I was most at home. I know now that I was a handful in those days.

There were only twenty-four pupils in the school altogether. There were only two in my class with me: Mary Moran and Big Jim O'Sullivan. The class below me had Jeddy O'Connor, Danny O'Sullivan, Louis Moran and the other Jim O'Sullivan, from the Randy.

The Randy Quay was a veritable haven where Eugey O'Sullivan and his wife Bridie reared their large family in hard-earned comfort at the estuary water's edge.

So, in October 1962, three ten year olds, Jeddy O'Connor, Danny O'Sullivan and Martin Ferris, led a strike for better conditions at Barrow School.

> They were all in that class and we hung around together. We called a strike over conditions at Barrow School. Danny, Jeddy and myself led the strike. We were only ten years old at the time. We made ridiculous demands, like two breaks per day for food and football, in addition to lunch break. We wanted less homework, a shorter day and the return of a retired female teacher. It was crazy childish stuff but a great challenge then at our age.

Martin's young reputation for taking on authority had spawned.

Martin Ferris has been instrumental in causing some significant entries to the history books, and, not surprisingly, he admits that he liked history at school, having a particular interest in that subject and mathematics.

> They were the two subjects at which I was reasonably good. Obviously I was good enough at maths because the teacher at Barrow school told my father when I was in fifth class that I was fairly good. She was a good teacher. She was one of the few teachers I really liked. She said that it would be better sending me to a school where there was a man because he would have more control over me. Mrs Griffin stressed to my father that what I needed was a male teacher to control me and that I was apparently very undisciplined at the time.
>
> So I went down to the Spa School to Master Jerry Brosnan, and he spent a year trying to put a bit of discipline into me. After that I went to the Green Christian Brothers Secondary School in Tralee, and

they spent about three years trying to put discipline into me, and when they wouldn't take any more, I went to the Technical School in Tralee.

In this school he went to the rescue of a frail, middle-aged teacher, Arnold Fanning, when a pupil struck the teacher. Ferris overpowered his classmate, thus saving Mr Fanning from further punishment. The wild kid was becoming a man, although still relatively untamed. He explains:

> At Tralee Technical School they spent about eight months trying to discipline me, and they failed as well. I got thrown out of there. I suppose you could say, I got expelled from three schools. I just rebelled against school – anything that was compulsory: the Irish language would to this day be very difficult for me. In prison life I never availed of the opportunity – it was a kind of a mental blockage for me. Anything that was imposed created a barrier, a blockage; it is a sign of possible stubbornness in me.

In 1962, when Martin was ten, Kerry was buzzing with football madness. Kerry had beaten Cork in the Munster Final by 4–8 to 0–4 and were into the All-Ireland Semi-Final. Martin Ferris had been in the packed Cork Athletic Grounds at the final. He had been showing distinct football promise at Barrow School and in other football fields around the parish. Reliable football judges had already pencilled him in as a potential Kerry footballer. He had fearless tenacity, strength, speed, hunger for the ball and "great hands". In Kerry of that era, good hands were vital for the type of game they played.

He remembers that Munster Final well. It had been a tempestuous decider. There were battles on the field and war off the pitch as a number of spectators took things a little seriously. The powerful Kerry number four, Tim Lyons, knocked out the formidable Cork midfielder, Garda Eric Ryan, in a robust session midway through the game.

Kerry number six, Noel Lucey, was sent off for a fracas with a number of Cork players, including Joe O'Sullivan, Gene McCarthy and Ned Coughlan. Kerry's star forward, Dan McAuliffe, was punched by a spectator after the match. The Kerry players, substitutes and selectors had to receive garda protection in the middle of the pitch. Still in their playing gear, they moved en masse towards their cars parked near the river Lee. One nasty incident saw a player's car, parked on the grassy-sloped bank of the river, being heaved dangerously towards the Lee by an enraged crowd. Garda intervention prevented a possible disaster. Famous Cork GAA personality Denis Conroy was pictured appealing to the vexed Cork crowd for calm during a particularly tough period in the match.

However, young Ferris remembers the game mostly for the fact that his younger brother Brian went walkabout and was announced over the loudspeakers as having been lost. The youngster was later discovered safe and sound when he was collected from high up in the broadcasting box after the game. It was a memorable first major sporting experience for young Martin.

With football excitement boiling over within Kerry, the youngsters had asked Patie to bring them over from their home in Barrow to Fenit, where they knew there would be a "few kicks" in progress at the Trough Field. So Patie dropped the boys off while he visited O'Sullivan's Bar in Fenit for a few drinks. It was not normal for Barrow people from across the little estuary to visit Fenit for football, although most of the older men worked on Fenit pier as part-time dockers and occasional fishermen. "While we could see across the estuary to Fenit, it was a fair old journey for youngsters to walk by road," recalls Martin.

The swallows were flying low on that humid summer evening at the Trough Field in Fenit. Midges pestered the twenty or so heavily sweating men and youths who jumped in two groups to secure the high flying football. One group stood in the "square" in front of the high, crooked, unpainted goalposts; the other group contested the lone battered football as it dropped from the sky outside in the middle of the pitch.

Another group of five or six youngsters spent some time fruitlessly following the feeding swallows as they dived and darted around the massed midges over the bare, well-grazed field. Martin and his brother Brian were amongst the younger group of boys who alternated from chasing the swallows to securing the odd catch and kick of a stray ball, miskicked by the two adult groups of enthusiastic footballers.

These were economically poor times. Few of those kicking football that summer evening possessed the slightest semblance of playing gear. Most were dressed in shirt and trousers and everyday shoes; in most cases, they would be wearing their only pair of shoes. A small few might have football boots and shorts. Mike Browne was there. He was one of the older fellows doing well for ball in the middle of the unmarked pitch. J.P. O'Sullivan, future detective garda, was at the time a very promising juvenile footballer, one of the few complete with football boots and togs. It was an innocent time in the sporting life of Ireland, and the scene mirrored thousands of similarly poor rural Gaelic football playing fields throughout the Ireland of the early 1960s. The football played was very rough-and-tumble stuff in that pitch, but it was great fun for young men.

The lives of these three boys, Mike Browne, Martin Ferris and J.P. O'Sullivan, were to cross almost a decade and a half later. Mike Slattery was on the field, too, and he would also become a garda in adult years. But on that clammy, midge-infested evening, nobody could guess or even care where it would all lead or where they would all end up.

And so began a lifelong interaction between the youngster from Barrow and the people of the village of Fenit, as football at the Trough Field became an almost regular pastime for the two young Ferris brothers from then on.

At Barrow Primary School, leadership qualities were already manifesting themselves in Martin as he organised football in the school. There were only ten boys in the area, but they decided to form a team and buy a set of football jerseys all by themselves. In those frugal times, the ability of parents to financially come to their aid for such unnecessary luxuries was unheard of, and so a scheme to pick periwinkles and sell them was hatched by the children. They duly raised enough money to fulfil their dream. When the day to purchase the jerseys dawned, the youngsters prevailed on a local farmer, John O'Connor of Knockanagh, to drive them all the way to a shop in Castleisland, almost twenty miles away from Barrow. That Saturday afternoon was a highlight in the life of at least ten budding young footballers from Barrow as they made their pilgrimage to Castleisland to purchase their first ever set of jerseys. The problem they encountered was one of quite serious proportions: the shop didn't have the blue colour with a white collar they wanted. So they decided amongst themselves to settle for the next best thing. They left that shop a proud and excited group of young footballers. And from that day forward the football jerseys of the boys from Barrow were to be green with a white collar.

Martin remembers the rivalry between the Spa National School team and his own team, Barrow National School:

> We went down then and we played in the Spa field. And even though I was going to the Spa National School, I played with Barrow National School. And now the Spa was a big school and Bawneen Stack was playing with them, and he was in seventh class in the Spa school at the time. He was a year older than us. And you had Denis O'Sullivan, you had the Hogans, Rory and Michael, and you had Timmy Moynihan. You had all of those lads and they were all good footballers. The Barrow lads had young Kirby, Big Jim Sullivan and myself and Jeddy O'Connor, Danny O'Sullivan and my brother Brian. And we picked our

team and we went down and we beat them below in the Spa. I'll never forget it. Mike Stack was refereeing it, and he would be fair to us and to himself. His brother Bawneen and himself had a row over some decision he made. Bawneen was going mad, of course. He gave the brother, the referee, a clatter. So there was mayhem. That was the first competitive match Barrow had ever played, in our era anyway.

The principal of the Spa National School, balding, tall and gruff Jerry Brosnan, was locally known as "the Master". He had a rough, aggressive demeanour with a bark much worse than his bite. He was football mad and was in charge of the Churchill parish team. The parish team encompassed the Spa, Fenit and Barrow when it played outside teams. Ferris remembers an early match:

> The Master said, "Fire in Ferris there!"
> I was mad for ball, and although I was playing at corner forward, I knew nothing about positional play and was following the ball everywhere it landed, all over the pitch. The Master shouted at me a few times to keep my position. But I kept chasing ball all over the place. Eventually the Master, who had found a bit of rope, ran into the pitch and shouted at me: "I'll tell you now, young Ferris, if you don't stay inside at corner forward, I'll tie that on to one of your legs and I'll drive a stake in the ground and you won't be able to move."

So, that was the first competitive match he ever played for Churchill parish.

Martin played in the Cotter Cup at under-14 age group. Football was becoming more organised at this period as competitions were regularised and there was more control by officialdom. However, this didn't prevent Ferris receiving a shiner from a partisan older umpire after he saved a certain goal shot under the crossbar in a Fenit v. the Spa challenge match.

Chapter One

I remember the umpire at one of my goalposts hit me a flake of a fist after I made a good save. I was playing in goals that night. I ended up with a fine black eye. Michael Lynch, Joeen O'Connell, the late Tommy "Tucker" Kelly,[1] the late Brian Kelly and Michael Lynch of Fenit were playing in that match. Michael Slattery was in charge of those games.

CHAPTER TWO

B Y THE AGE of thirteen, Martin Ferris was blazing a
trail through the juvenile football ranks. He had his
mind firmly set on winning a Kerry jersey as soon as
at all possible. He was also becoming aware of a world
beyond his own childhood one. He recalls one incident
around this time that had a significant impact on him.

It was a miserably cold, wet day. A south-easterly drove
the rain into their faces as Martin, his brother Brian and
their pals made their way back to Barrow from Ardfert
football field. As they approached Barney Brook Bridge,
the banter suddenly stopped. A shocking scene presented
itself before them. There, on the familiar green patch of
grass on the side of the road before you came to the bridge,
was a flimsy, patched-up canvas tent erected on the sodden
grass. A perished young tinker couple, now called travellers, were obviously using this as cover from the dreadful winter weather. The couple were settling themselves
down for the night as the woman pottered around on her
knees, half in and half out of the tent.

Chapter Two

Martin can remember it as if it were yesterday. The tent was constructed in the shape of a tunnel and could be entered at both ends. It consisted of a mere canvas sheet slung over a ridge pole suspended by ribs of sally rods about three or four feet off the drenched ground. The young, but already weather-beaten man was trying to warm himself by a struggling campfire, which he tried to encourage with bits of kindling sticks in front of the makeshift tent. The youngster could see that their bed was a tattered old canvas ground sheet. For Martin it was unbelievable that human beings could be exposed to such conditions. It was a shocking realisation. He was seeing poverty he never thought existed.

He stopped to talk to them. He had never met travellers before. It struck him as odd that his nervous pals cautioned him away from the young couple. Society bred a fear of these travelling people at the time. In fact, Ferris believes that this fear and mistrust was mutual between society and the travellers. One way or the other, it was on that day that the sense of inequality in society was impressed on him for the first time. "I just knew it was wrong."

Up to that he thought everybody was as skint for a few bob as he was, and that everybody had the struggles with crops and cows and pigs as did his father and mother and Brian and himself.

"Envy might possibly have been my sensation had I witnessed two people in front of a country campfire on a bright summer day, but under these atrocious conditions, the feeling was that of utter bewilderment and hopeless sorrow."

When Martin was fourteen, he and his family moved two miles from Barrow House to a scenic farm which Patie had bought at Churchill Cross, near Paddy O'Sullivan's forge, the parish church and the cemetery.

During Martin's teenage years of the 1960s, there was unfolding a movement for equality and civil rights in the USA. The advance of this movement was being shown on RTÉ news programmes on the fledgling national television network, which had been launched in 1962. Viewers witnessed violent hatred perpetrated against black protesters in such places as Selma, Alabama, in 1966. They were seeking "one man one vote", equality of education and an end to daily overt discrimination in American society. Martin Luther King Jr was rattling the cage of American politics in his campaign for equality and desegregation. It is inconceivable now to think that not just ordinary black people were subject to segregation but even the much-admired black star performers and great sports people, from Sammy Davis Jr to Nat King Cole to Ella Fitzgerald and Mohammed Ali. They could not sleep in a white hotel, use a white restaurant or choose where they sat on public transport. Concurrently, the little-known Nelson Mandela and the African National Congress (ANC) were also involved in a movement to rid South Africa of the outrageous apartheid system.

A little later in that decade in the north of Ireland, a movement calling for civil rights began to take shape. Here too were obvious inequalities, and a small group of peaceful, thinking people decided to highlight these violations imposed by the unionist ruling class. Out of this movement developed the Northern Ireland Civil Rights Association (NICRA). This movement was attempting to bring about an end to the historically blatant religious discrimination in employment and housing, corrupt policing and the gerrymandered political system that kept the Catholic/nationalist population down. NICRA hoped that peaceful protest might bring about their dream of change too. In hindsight, it appears that in the face of such unionist intransigence and gerrymandering they never really had a chance.

In one striking example of religious discrimination, in 1969 the County Fermanagh Educational Committee employed seventy-seven school-bus drivers. In this county, which had a Catholic majority, only three of the seventy-seven were Catholics. Nowhere in Europe was such rampant discrimination openly practised.

While the Catholic/nationalist population simply sought civil rights that were afforded to all British citizens, the vociferous Protestant leader Ian Paisley's message was to deny them everything. He carried his violent rhetoric of hatred of Catholics on to the streets, proclaiming "not an inch". When Catholics reacted, they were driven off the streets by the pro-British, Protestant, armed paramilitary force known as the B Specials. This brutal force combined with the Royal Ulster Constabulary to form a cocktail of hatred-based armed power capable of maintaining a disenfranchised and downtrodden Catholic population. Unionism was an ideology that thrived on a sense of siege. Even the confidence of knowing that the gerrymandered political system guaranteed them a virtually permanent majority could not overcome a deep sense of political psychosis. There would be no hand of friendship or co-operation from the vast majority of Protestants.

On 4 January 1969, a peaceful People's Democracy march was ambushed and violently beaten down at Burntollet Bridge in Derry. Their concerted attackers were loyalists and off-duty RUC members, B Specials and Paisley-organised supporters. The People's Democracy marchers were unarmed, and, through television, the attack was witnessed by a world which had seen similar action taken by white racists against Dr King and his supporters in the Selma to Montgomery march in Alabama, and elsewhere. The world was outraged at the horrific footage.

The seventeen-year-old Martin Ferris watched the savage attack on television, and it was also to have a lasting effect on him to see peaceful men and women mercilessly baton-charged on that day.

"For the first time, through the advent of television, we were able to see the terrible things that were happening to our people on the streets, to the Civil Rights Movement and so forth. It was justifying everything that local republican Mick Lynch had been telling us all along. That British presence of maintaining and propping up, and collaborating in the institutionalising of inequality between unionists and nationalists, was always going to cause problems."

Under intense pressure from the Wilson government in London, with rioting on the streets and the scenario of power collapsing around him, northern Prime Minister Terence O'Neill went for the enormous step of introducing "one man, one vote" on 22 April 1969. The full parliamentary party accepted the change by twenty-eight votes to twenty-two. Brian Faulkner voted against. However, on 28 April, O'Neill was forced to resign under the threat of impending defeat at a meeting of the Unionist Party Standing Committee. On 1 May 1969, his cousin, another unionist "grandee", Major Chichester-Clarke, succeeded him as leader of the Unionist Party.

On 9 May 1969, the Unionist Party Standing Committee accepted the principle of "one man, one vote". On 21 May, Chichester-Clarke and Brian Faulkner led a delegation to Downing Street where they saw British Prime Minister Harold Wilson and Home Secretary James Callaghan. Wilson announced that the next local elections in the Six Counties would be held under "one man, one vote".

In O'Neill's resignation speech on television, he said: "I have tried to break the chains of ancient hatreds. I have been unable to realise during my period of office all that I had sought to achieve. Whether now it can be achieved in my lifetime I do not know. But one day these things will be and must be achieved."[1]

Leading members of a socialist-inclined IRA at that time were trying to take the gun out of politics. In December 1969, a major upheaval amongst republicans saw an impending split develop. Some socialists amongst them, some with Marxist inclinations, were seen to be controlling republicanism under the direction of Cathal Goulding and others. Southern republicans had numerical control of the ruling executive. It was felt that the unarmed nationalist population had been left exposed and defenceless during the riots of the previous year. Although dominated by personnel from south of the border, a breakaway, more militant arm of republicanism was founded under the direction of Seán Mac Stiofáin, Ruairí Ó Brádaigh, Dáithí Ó Conaill, John Joe McGirl and others. Word of the split and formation of the rival IRA was leaked to the press in late December 1969. Confirming the story, the new group claimed that a majority of IRA units had sworn allegiance to the Provisional Army Council and Executive of the IRA. On the streets of Belfast and Derry, the popular name "Provisionals" stuck and was shortened to the widely used "Provos". As a consequence, Goulding's faction became known as the Official IRA. However, there was no doubt the Provisionals had arrived on the stage in the Six Counties.

In the Republic, from 1969 onwards, Kerry was probably the most active county in the support for the armed struggle of the IRA against the British. Such was the strength and depth of the republican tradition in the county.

Kerry had taken its share of hardship during the War of Independence and the Civil War. The Fenit/Spa/ Churchill area would have seen much action in Easter Week but for a mix-up in dispatches and the loss of the arms shipment from the German ship the *Aud*. Republican activist Roger Casement, who was involved in the abortive arms shipment plan, came ashore in a small punt from a German submarine and was captured behind Banna Strand, near Ardfert. He was taken by rail from Tralee to Dublin and onwards by ship to London, where he was hanged in August 1916.

After the Easter Rising in 1916, a general roundup of republicans by the British saw a number of Kerrymen deported for incarceration in Frongoch, Wales.[2]

Kerry also suffered from a heavy Black and Tan presence during the War of Independence. The infamous and dreaded Auxiliary Major MacKinnon created havoc in his travels around Kerry until he was shot dead while playing golf in Tralee on 15 April 1921. He had shot two IRA men, Maurice Reidy and John Leen, dead in cold blood at Ballymacelligott on Christmas Eve, 1920. On 14 May, a month after Mac Kinnon's killing, the RIC head constable, Francis Benson, was shot dead in Pembroke Street, Tralee. As a result, during a strict curfew, many homes and businesses of republicans were burned to the ground by the British. On 1 June 1921, a cycle patrol of Black and Tans led by a District Inspector McCaughey of the RIC was ambushed by the IRA outside Castlemaine village, near Tralee, County Kerry. There were only two survivors from the nine-man patrol. Sadly, the Truce was only weeks away.

The first official shots in the War of Independence are recognised as having been fired at Soloheadbeg in County Tipperary on 21 January 1919. However, on 13 April 1918, the Gortatlea RIC Barracks outside Tralee was attacked, and local volunteers Richard Laide and John Browne lost their lives as a result. Kerry had obviously fired the first shots.

In Mick Lynch's pub in the Spa, Martin Ferris heard such stories, and through Liam Cotter and old republican Paddy Crean he gleaned the information and cultivated a devoted interest in the republican struggle north of the border.

> Mick Lynch, for as long as I can remember, was the face of Irish republicanism in the area when I was young, along with my cousin, Jack Ferris of Ballyea, who was known as Ace, and Paddy Crean. These were the three people that I can remember as republicans at that time. Ace Ferris once threw his coat over a table covered with ammunition as an unsuspecting Garda Sergeant Hickey of Fenit paid him a friendly visit and sat down to drink a mug of tea with him. My first memory of Mick Lynch goes back to the Border Campaign of 1956–57. My father sold potatoes to shops in Tralee and Castleisland, and I

would always be with him when he went delivering them. My father would carry me everywhere with him as a kid. I remember I was with him delivering to Porter's Shop in Castleisland (it's no longer there), when we heard President Kennedy had been shot dead. These things stay in your mind. He'd seldom pass Lynch's, on our way home. He would usually have a bottle of beer, of Black Label. He wasn't a heavy drinker, but if he went to the pub at night it would be for a half-one and a couple of bottles of Black Label.

In 1957 on one of those nights returning from selling potatoes, Patie Ferris paid a visit to Mick Lynch for a drink. It was after Sinn Féin had tasted considerable success in the 1957 general election with John Joe Rice elected in South Kerry and three others also elected to Leinster House on a Sinn Féin abstentionist policy. There were some *United Irishman* newspapers, then the organ of Sinn Féin, for sale on the counter, and Patie Ferris bought a copy.

Mick Lynch and Patie Ferris would have had much in common from the farming point of view. Lynch, as well as owning the pub, grew early potatoes and kept a handful of pigs. In other words, he could also be classified as a very small farmer. Politically, Lynch and Patie Ferris had different ideological slants. Although both had socialist tendencies, the republican political link would gradually be forged instead with Martin.

Mick Lynch's pub was traditionally a safe republican house. Down the years many republicans from north and south of the border who were on the run or just having a break from the harsh conditions up there sampled the hospitality of Mick and Ellen Lynch and family. The bar enjoyed a thriving rural business that made it a welcoming centre for much activity in the parish. It was the home of the Kerries and Knockanish Greyhound Coursing Club. Each Sunday of the winter, from 1 October to 1 March, a sixteen-dog Open Coursing Stake was run off over the open fields of the Kerries and Knockanish countryside. Afterwards the "beaters", dog owners and club members adjourned to Mick Lynch's for nourishment in front of a well-stoked open turf fire. The pub was also the unofficial home base of the Spa-Churchill Gaelic football club.

From about 1968 on, I would be in the Spa three or four nights a week playing football. We would cycle down, play our football, go to Lynch's for a bottle of Cidona and a bag of Taytos, and then cycle home again to Churchill or Barrow. During the summer we would be playing every night. Sometimes just Batt O'Shea and myself, just belting a ball in and out, from one to the other. Then we started drinking down there. When I was about sixteen, I started drinking for the first time. Like every young fellow we would try to sneak a half pint or so on the quiet.

I remember being in Lynch's when Belfast Sinn Féin Councillor Máire Moore was recuperating there after being shot in the leg. I remember Jim Bryson being there after escaping from the *Maidstone* prison ship. He was there with Alec Crowe, who did life in the H Blocks afterwards. Alec was a brilliant fellow to explain the reason behind the struggle and what it entailed. He never glorified violence. He said the whole thing was about justice. He was a lovely man to talk to. I felt very comfortable with him. Jim Bryson lost his life with fellow IRA volunteer Paddy Mulvenna while on active service. At the time it was believed locally that the Official IRA were responsible for their deaths. However this suspicion was without foundation.

Lynch's was a great safe house. Gerry Adams's brother Paddy and his wife spent their honeymoon at Lynch's in 1971 or '72. John Murphy of Blackpool, the Spa, and myself picked them up from Banteer Station during the European election or something like that. I'd say a great number of prominent republicans found sanctuary in Lynch's. I remember Máire Drumm and her daughter, young Máire, staying there. Proinsias Mac Art, Sean Keenan, Richard Behal, Kevin Hannaway, Liam Hannaway, Seán Mac Stiofáin, Ruairí Ó Brádaigh and Walter Ó Loinsigh, amongst the many.

I was meeting a great many strong republicans through Mick Lynch. He could never be intimidated by Special Branch pressure and would just laugh off any suggestions or accusations.

During those years my father was paying back a big slice of money to the bank for the land he bought. It was big money that time. I think he paid £1,600 for Walsh's farm. It was £100 an acre, and then he bought thirty-six acres in Carmody's farm for which he paid £6,000, and that too was big money at that time. He sold some to a rich sister of his, and the proceeds from that sale eased the burden considerably.

Martin's father died in 1970 at the age of sixty-five years of age. Patie had been taking medication for some time for high blood pressure. Then one Friday evening while Brian and Martin were milking the cows, Patie got what turned out to be a slight stroke. The doctor was called and the two sons finished off the last few cows before Martin drove his father to hospital in Tralee. While they were doing tests on his father, he drove on eleven miles to Castleisland to play an important Minor County Championship match against John Mitchell's Club, Tralee. Pat Keohane, son of Martin's great friend Joe, and Martin were sent off for fighting shortly after half-time. He returned to the hospital immediately and was told that his father had settled down. He looked fine but his speech was impaired. He died eight days later on 26 May after suffering another stroke. There was a big parish funeral, but immediately it was over Martin, Brian and some uncles had to go to the fields to attend to a substantial crop of onions. Martin decided to join the IRA on the day his father was buried.

"I was just turned eighteen. His death was a terrible blow to us. We had just enough to get by in those times. We lived off Mary Joe's book. It was the custom in those times. There was nobody rich in our area, but there was really nobody very poor either. We thought everybody was the same. You lived from season to season with Mary Joe's credit book in her little shop near Chapeltown Creamery. She was a great neighbour."

Things were very hard when his father died, but his mother overcame all of that too.

"She was an unbelievably strong woman for such a frail-looking little person. She was very cagey with money and would walk the town for a bargain. She would make a small amount go very far indeed."

They had hard times in that they lived from season to season between the earnings from sea and the land. In autumn the oyster bed provided a boost to the coffers. Christmas was good because they had the money from the beet crop too. But that would be gone by the spring, and they had most of March, April and half of May without a penny coming into the house. And then when they sold the potatoes, they had to pay Mary Joe's book. When they got right through selling the potatoes, they had the corn, and of course there was always a couple of litters of bonhams (piglets) in the farm. This was the life being carved out from the land and the sea for Martin Ferris.

When Patie Ferris died there was £600 owing to the bank. The teenagers and their mother were intent on clearing off any debts due by their father, and Martin can still account for how that was achieved:

> There was a quarter of an acre of onion sets which yielded six tonne three hundredweights, and at £100 per tonne it produced £630, which was considerable money in 1970. You wouldn't get it for onions today. We sold them over in Milltown, and my mother took the money into Tralee and paid off the bank. My father died in May and the onions were done in the

first week in July. Five weeks after he died. It was pity that he didn't live long enough to have the financial pressure off him.

We had great neighbours in farming that time. I remember when my father died it was 26 May. After his funeral my Uncle Euge, who came from England, and the other brothers, Mautie and Jack, and John Lawlor and Sonny Lawlor and myself hoed about five acres of Kerrs Pinks potatoes.

It was all done in a couple of days, and they turned out to be a fine crop.

Apart from the daily milking there was nothing urgent to do then but wait for the beet to come through and the oyster fishing to begin in October. Martin remembers the pride in farming at that time. There probably is still great pride in farming, but at that time there was greater concentration on quality rather than quantity. There was a competitive pride in the neighbourhood in having good floury spuds. There was a real satisfaction in having the potatoes "sat" and the crops blessed. The blessing of the crops was a big thing.

All of this Martin can remember well, from the start in the morning with the cows and right through the day. It was many the day that Danny O'Sullivan and himself discussed these pleasant times from home when they were both prisoners in Portlaoise Prison.

> You started in the morning with the milking of the cows. Then you went to the creamery where you would have a chat with the neighbours. Back home then on the tractor to wash the milk tanks and have a bit of breakfast. The day was spent tending to other chores like crops and animals before driving in the cows at 5.30 again for the second milking. That would be finished and cows let out again by 7 to 7.30. I would be rushing off to the football field then for training. If there was no training, you would love

to walk down the gardens at 8 or 9 o'clock, in summertime, especially, to check the crops. You would be checking the stalks and measuring how high they were up to your leg, compared to the same time the previous years. All of those little things made farming a very pleasant life.

Everything around farming that time was simple. So simple, even the sprays we used. We used bluestone and washing soda and some other mixture to combat blight on the spuds. Nowadays the chemicals are gone away too strong. This might have improved the quantity but not the quality. I remember for the early potatoes we would draw seaweed up from the beach and we'd line the furrow with the seaweed. Then we would put a case of potatoes on top of it and then close the furrow. When the stalks came up you would pinch the nitrate that was alongside the stalk. Now the chemicals are all spreading wild. We were probably using far less artificial manure than they would be using now. We would put out farmyard dung and spread it at the end of the year, and that would soak into the ground to nourish it for the following planting season. There was a lot of natural fertilizer used then. You wouldn't use much nitrate because the more nitrate you used the more artificial your potatoes would be. As a result the quality would suffer and the spuds would be less floury and not as good for eating.

Martin's friend Donal Devane produced great potatoes. He took pride in his fine spuds. He grew Pickers and British Queens. Martin grew Home Guard and Kerrs Pink, but the British Queens would come in after the early crop and before the main crop. Donal always had his own market for his potatoes. They were very special, and he did well from them. In some parts of Kerry a man was judged by how high he could jump to catch a football; in other cases it would be how good a ploughman or fisherman he was; but Dan Devane, he was known well for producing good early spuds.

The month of May 1970 was a turbulent period on the whole island of Ireland. There was consternation in the Dublin government when Taoiseach Jack Lynch sacked two senior government ministers. On the morning of 6 May 1970, the national newspapers screamed astonishing headlines at the Irish people. Jack Lynch had fired the minister for finance, Charles Haughey, and the minister for agriculture, Neil Blaney. A third senior minister, Kevin Boland, minister for local government, and a junior minister, Paudge Brennan, resigned. The country was in crisis amid a story of arms importation by ministers and further stories of the dreadful hardship being suffered by the nationalist population in the Six Counties. It troubled and frightened a great many people in the south. Most looked to their government for direction. Others looked to people of action for a way in which the suffering witnessed on television, in places such as Belfast and Derry, could be alleviated. In that fateful month of May 1970, young Martin Ferris cared and he took the trouble to ask the questions.

Martin's cousin Jack "Ace" Ferris had been a republican and had spent nearly five years interned in the Curragh prison camp during the 1940s. He was to forge in Martin an early interest in Irish republicanism. Martin also had a deep interest in Irish history; it was his favourite subject in school. He had always felt that Britain never had a right to be in any part of Ireland. And now, with the advent of television, Martin could see with his own eyes the direct result of partition and Britain's involvement in Ireland's affairs. In 1969 he had seen hundreds of Catholics being burned out of their homes in Bombay Street in Belfast. He saw loyalists and the sectarian B-Specials, side by side, attacking nationalists during the Battle of the Bogside in Derry. He witnessed, along with the rest of Ireland, the civil rights movement, whose only demand was one person-one vote, being beaten off the streets. Now wasn't a time for words: action was needed, and Martin wasn't willing to stand idly by while this suffering continued.

The psychological conditioning of young Ferris as a republican was taking shape. The control exercised by his father's discipline for hard work was not present any more, and so Martin was a free agent to exercise his devotion to republican values and the cause for relief of the suffering in the Six Counties. The biggest decision of his life was about to be made. The north was in chaos and southern politics in a very tenuous situation. As a young man of action, Ferris took what he saw as the only course open to him.

Martin had been influenced towards republicanism first by Mick Lynch, but now he was approached by two well known republicans and asked if he would be prepared to help out the struggle. "My father died on 26 May 1970; I joined the republican struggle on 29 May 1970."

He was sworn in by Paddy Kelly, a painting contractor from Ardfert, and Liam Cotter, former vice-chairman of Kerry County Board of the GAA. Kelly had worked abroad before returning and settling in Kerry. He was quite active behind the scenes. Liam Cotter was a more conspicuous figure in republicanism. His mother was a cousin of the legendary John Joe Sheehy.

If his work-orientated father Patie had not died in May 1970, would Martin have had the freedom to join the IRA and devote so much of his time to the struggle? Patie Ferris was a tough taskmaster, and Martin would have had to work hard on the farm. He might not have been afforded the time to involve himself so deeply in republicanism.

Martin recalls his father's attitude towards hard work in a few words: "I would go oyster fishing with him on a Saturday when we didn't have school. We would be hauling the dredge by hand, but my dad would never cut the engine. He would get a great kick out of our appeals to him to make it easier on us."

The IRA in Munster was designated responsibility for providing funds for the struggle to support the IRA activity in the Six Counties and England. This entailed the provision of personnel, either in the north or in England, supply lines for arms and explosives, factories where active service volunteers produced explosives and, of course, funds from armed raids. In the north of Ireland, hundreds of men were being interned and scores killed by the British army and RUC. As a suspected volunteer, Ferris was thought by the authorities to be involved in much of the activity surrounding the garnering of such funds.

There were a number of armed operations in the Munster area after which an accusing finger was pointed at Ferris. It was during a period when the ideals impressed on Martin by Mick Lynch and many friends from the north would be fully tested. He also had quite an amount of football appetite to fill over the ensuing years. It was not an easy time for him or for the Special Branch members charged with his surveillance. Keeping as close an eye as possible on the busy youth, the Branch visited his casual workplace on building sites, the farm, his home, football training and matches on a number of occasions each day. Over the years his mother learned to live with the regular visits and searches for her busy sons.

In 1972 the parish team of Churchill won the Kerry County Novice Championship, and Ferris was one of the driving forces in the great campaign. Bringing massive pride to the parish, he teamed up well at centre half-forward with future Kerry midfielder Pat McCarthy. On the route to the final there were some stormy contests, but they won the first ever championship for the parish of Spa-Churchill, and so every member of the team became a hero. The bond between the players played a major part in the victory. Ferris was the leader, and to this day there is a strong camaraderie between all of those players involved.[3]

Now it seemed only a matter of time before a Kerry jersey would find its way on to the shoulders of twenty-year-old

Ferris. He was called into action with the Kerry Under-21 squads and scored the winning goal when Kerry beat Cork in the Munster Under-21 Final in 1972. He went on to line out at full forward in the All-Ireland Under-21 Final of the same year when Kerry lost to Galway by 2–6 to 0–7.

But by now, with his committment to Kerry football clashing with his IRA involvement, holding down a constant place on the team proved difficult. Sometimes he was on the run from the law and could not risk exposure on a football pitch. He was generally operating elsewhere in the Munster area and unavailable for training and matches in Kerry. Visits from the Special Branch made it difficult for him to live with his mother and Brian at home in Churchill. With it becoming increasingly difficult for him to sleep at home all of the time, his fitness for football at top level suffered.

A disused, uninhabitable house in the vicinity of his home, where he had only the rats and rooks for company, became one of his regular billets when being sought by the law. He would have to evacuate his accommodation at about 6 a.m. each morning, as it was from that time onwards that the Special Branch raided. He would watch from a distance in the fields as they raided his home or billet. When the coast was clear, he would go to his mother for breakfast.

Garda intelligence seemed to place him in many hot spots, but at this stage nothing concrete could be confirmed against him. It was known locally that he was involved with republicanism to a certain degree, but few knew exactly to what extent. However, there was a certain wildness and courage about the young man they called "Pony", a nickname earned when the long-haired youngster unnoticingly carried an opposing player on his back while solo running through a defence with the football. Many older and conservative people believed his swashbuckling recklessness would lead the same Pony into serious trouble.

By 1973, appearances for the Kerry Under-21 team would be arranged by himself and former Kerry football great Joe Keohane, who was also a Kerry selector and a very strong republican. Keohane was to remain a close friend. Fellow Kerry team selector, and republican, John Joe Sheehy was also in on the arrangements, which were similar to those that had been made for Sheehy as a young player on the run in the 1920s.

For the Under-21 All-Ireland Semi-Final in Tralee in 1973, it was decided by them that, with an eye to security, it would be more sensible if Ferris did not line out at corner forward as per the official programme. Ferris, in hooded anorak, discreetly watched as Kerry struggled through to earn a place against Mayo in the All-Ireland Final. Standing incognito on the crowded terrace, Ferris had to listen to some members of the crowd standing near him shouting abuse at young Michael O'Shea, who was wearing Martin's number 13 jersey and who did not have a particularly good match: "Come on, Ferris, get into it! Wake up!" However, with that game eventually won, Ferris would be available to be sprung from the substitutes' bench in the All-Ireland Final against Mayo, played in Ennis.

Cusack Park, Ennis, was thronged on Sunday, 16 September. The geographical situation of the Clare capital comfortably suited those travelling from both participating counties. As the rain teemed down, Mayo raced into what seemed like an unassailable lead of 0–9 to 0–1 at half-time. Many rain-soaked followers from both counties decided to head for the exits – Mayo supporters ecstatic at winning and Kerry followers disgusted at their team's dismal first-half performance. Ferris was duly sprung from the bench. *The Kerryman* newspaper reported: "Ferris certainly upset Mayo around the square when he went in, and this meant a great deal to the victory effort."

The sports editor of *The Kerryman*, John Barry, is a good judge of the game, but in those words he could be deemed to have understated. From the moment the long-haired

Ferris arrived on to the pitch to his marker, John O'Mahony (later of Galway team management fame), the spirit began to pump again in the heart of Kerry players. Things had seemed hopeless for Kerry. Now the fire that Kerry needed was supplied by Ferris, and it was no coincidence that the mayhem he caused around the Mayo full-back line allowed two of the greatest forwards ever, Mikey Sheehy and John Egan, the space to defeat Mayo.

Many good judges of the game maintained that Ferris was instrumental in getting the vital touch leading to one of these goals. On that talented team with Sheehy and Egan, Kerry also had Ger Power and Paidí Ó Sé. Collectively the four would win thirty senior medals. Power, Sheehy and Ó Sé each won a record eight All-Ireland Senior Football Championship medals. The team also had the great Paudie Lynch, who on that occasion was having an atypically poor game. He was eventually called ashore, probably for the only time in his career. Current Fine Gael TD Jimmy Deenihan was on that team too, as were other stars of that golden era: Ger O'Keeffe, Paudie O'Mahony, Tim Kennelly and captain Micky Ned O'Sullivan. Martin's great friend and club mate, Batt O'Shea, was the star defender on that memorable occasion.

Martin and Batt celebrated the great victory for a number of days afterwards in the company of their friends at Mick Lynch's pub in the Spa. Many of the players who won Kerry's second ever Under-21 All-Ireland title went on to become household names in the history of Gaelic football.

Mick O'Dwyer, who is arguably the greatest Gaelic football personality in the 120-year history of Gaelic games, says of Ferris: "I have no doubt that Martin would have won many All-Ireland senior football medals if he had given football his 100 per cent concentration. He had everything we would look for in a star player."

However, although Ferris enjoyed the flush of victory, it was now evident to him that his football career would have to be put on ice for a time. When Batt O'Shea and himself arrived back to Mick Lynch's on the Monday after the Under-21 victory, Ferris handed his own medal across the counter to Mick's daughter Áine, asking her to mind it for him. It was symbolic. He had other things to do now.

Shortly afterwards, Ferris got a run out with the Kerry senior team against Laois in Portlaoise town. He scored three goals and two points in that challenge game. Happy at having played well in that match, he pondered the idea of giving more time to training. However, he could not successfully mix IRA activities with sport, as well as his work on the farm and out fishing, and so he decided his first allegiance could not be to football.

The Gaelic name for Fenit is Fianait. It can mean wild place, an accurate enough description considering the winds that come in off the Atlantic and up through Tralee Bay. The young men who lived in that area in the 1970s epitomised the name of their village. They were mainly fishermen, harvesting the wild Atlantic. They were wild, hard-living men too. Ferris was amongst them. Martin certainly had little regard for man-made laws during those years. But neither had many of the young men from around the Fenit and Churchill area.

From Fenit up Tralee Bay to the Spa and across to Derrymore beach on the Dingle Peninsula, there is a rich harvest of oysters every year from October to March. It was quietly harvested for years by two boats, one of which was operated by former local War of Independence IRA leader Micky Moriarty and his sons Jack and Mikey. The other boat was operated by Dan Crowley and his brother William. Over the years the two boat owners made a good living from "the bed", until a few naive younger fishermen allowed news of a bonanza to spread to the airwaves. Within a season or two, the number of boats doubled, then trebled, until the figure grew to an incredible 120. This duly resulted in the exploitation of the young oyster, threatening to destroy the oyster bed for ever. Trouble was brewing in the oyster fishing industry, and Martin Ferris became one of the leading spokesmen of the local fishermen.

From the times of RIC rule and down the decades since 1923, the barracks in Fenit had been staffed by up to four policemen. In the 1960s it was decided first to reduce the local force to one garda and then to close the station and police Fenit by garda squad car from Tralee. This meant that normal policing of the parish was now being done from moving cars. Where once everybody knew the local gardaí, now they were dealing with outsiders. The personal contact was lost. Now, the youth of the area were being policed by a squad car full of strangers, with contact limited to the official-duty kind. It is fair to wonder if this contributed to the growing resentment developing between the local young people and the Tralee gardaí. The Spa, closer to Tralee, produced a more law-abiding group of young men, but at the same time Ferris was a unifying factor between each of the areas. The parish was united behind him, both as an outspoken local leader in the oyster bed trouble and as a football hero.

As a republican he gradually became identifiable as a member of colour parties and as a speaker at republican gatherings. He could be seen in black beret and paramilitary uniform at republican funerals and commemorations.

Unhelpful to his reputation was one occasion when things turned very sour and got quite out of hand. On a windy night in 1974 at Tralee Sailing Club in Fenit, a group of young local men were refused admission to a bar extension. Two or three officials on the door proclaimed no entry, and evidence in the Circuit Court disclosed that one man spat in the face of Ferris. There was quite an amount of drink involved, as the local men had been drinking heavily after coming in from fishing. This brought about an uncharacteristically immature response from the twenty-two year old. It resulted in a court case in Killarney.

Chapter Two

Weekend problems with the squad car began to be a common enough occurrence. There was an almost constant presence of garda squad cars in the area by then. Christmas Eve was usually a boisterous night in the parish as too many young men, normally pint drinkers, drank whiskey or red rum for probably the only night in the year, causing the much-loved old parish priest, Fr Eugene O'Connor, to change the times of masses to bring midnight mass forward to ten o'clock and even nine o'clock, to avoid pub closing time.

But the boys still had enough time in the pub before fulfilling their religious duties. On one of these occasions in which the garda squad car from Tralee arrived outside the church in Fenit to question some of the local young men, the gardaí were unable to leave their vehicle. A crowd of locals had surrounded it, pressing their bodies against the doors. During this period, the resentment had grown to a point where the young men of the area would not cooperate with the gardaí in any circumstances, even when gardaí themselves were being investigated.

An investigation was begun into late drinking by two on-duty gardaí when a squad car visited Fenit on an August Saturday night. In hindsight it must appear quite comical. The two on-duty gardaí in charge became overly exuberant during a sing-song in a bar, contributing to the party atmosphere with a couple of songs themselves, as the "Garda" sign shone brightly on the roof of their Ford Zephyr parked fairly indiscreetly outside the bar. A garda cap went missing, and unfortunately for the two members that night, their car failed to take a bend at the Spa-Churchill crossroads on the way home. It was badly damaged when it struck a traffic sign.

An intensive enquiry by third-party gardaí and officers from the Garda Depot in Dublin never managed to get the local people to disclose the sing-song, the suspected reason for the crash or where the garda cap was to eventually hang itself. The Fenit people saw and heard nothing that night. It seems the local IRA gained a valuable cap which, it was rumoured, was afterwards used in some IRA activity, supplementing garda uniforms removed from the Fenit barracks at another time.

From autumn of 1974 to April 1975, Ferris underwent one of the most testing periods of his young life. He was on the run in the Munster area and was suspected of involvement in IRA activity. Despite undergoing heavy interrogation when eventually captured, Ferris did not break. All the Special Branch could successfully charge him with was membership of the IRA after he was eventually arrested. This first jail sentence was to harden even more the convictions of the resolute twenty-three year old as he became closer to some of the most unapologetic republicans in the island of Ireland. His own reputation as one who could take the pain associated with being a rebellious prisoner in Portlaoise Prison would gather momentum over the coming months of his first stint in jail.

At that time Martin's brother Brian would have been actively cooperative with many of Martin's actions. Although their mother must have suffered inwardly during these months, she never wilted in her support for her sons and was well aware of their activities. She relied on her religion through attendance at her daily nine o'clock mass at Churchill and maintained an outwardly brave acceptance of her problems.

In September 1974, the IRA raided Tralee Post Office and got away with £74,000, the largest haul recorded by the IRA in the south up to that time. Two well-known sports personalities masterminded the operation and the eventual safe passage of the funds to the Six Counties. It was one of the consignments known as smelly money, because it had been buried in a dung heap before being transported northwards. Although it was wrapped in plastic, the dampness of the dung seeped through. It got to Belfast anyway, smell and all.

Brendan O'Doherty, an IRA volunteer, was arrested in

connection with the raid. After intense interrogation at Tralee Garda Station, he was taken to Dublin by helicopter. A statement that Brendan alleged was extracted under torture was the only evidence produced in court; he was, however, convicted and sentenced to eight years in Portlaoise Prison. Newspapers reported that Ferris was the leader of the operation. Both he and Danny O'Sullivan were now firmly on the run and living away from home.

On one occasion, with Danny O'Sullivan, Martin survived in a hayshed in the Munster area for almost two weeks on a diet of a bottle of tea and ham sandwiches provided by the friendly but very nervous farmer who owned the hayshed. A spotter plane hovered overhead continuously for three days without detecting the two IRA volunteers. When rescued from that hayshed situation, Danny O'Sullivan and himself were taken to the home of John and Louise O'Carroll. Martin will never forget the welcome afforded to them by his friends, although the two IRA volunteers were infested with fleas and lice from the hay. The luxury of a hot bath and a clean bed is something Martin has never forgotten. Louise produced a large plate of ham sandwiches as a treat for the hungry men, not knowing that their diet for the past two weeks had also been ham sandwiches. It was a welcome light moment for all concerned.

The biggest robbery up to now had been the £74,000 taken from Tralee GPO in September. However, in the following December, during Christmas week, a raid on the Chase Manhattan Bank in Shannon was to yield a massive £159,000 for the northern cause. It raised the bar again in successul robberies, as the Shannon operation was now a new record heist. Fisherman Ferris was again suspected of making the haul. But the Special Branch would have to wait out the winter before having a chance to interrogate the Kerryman for both Tralee GPO and Shannon.

On 23 January 1975, there was an armed robbery on Central Dairies in Dungarvan, County Waterford. Ferris was suspected of operating in the Waterford/Cork area at the time. Garda activity was naturally intense as a result. On 14 February, three weeks after the raid, Detective Garda J.P. O'Sullivan of Union Quay Garda Station in Cork city and Detective Garda Ward got on the scent of Martin Ferris in Youghal, County Cork. There they joined up with two other detective gardaí, Murphy and McNulty, searching for suspects. Detective Garda J.P. O'Sullivan's sworn statement graphically explains how he arrested three suspected IRA volunteers on that St Valentine's Day.

I am a member of Detective Branch stationed at Union Quay, Garda Station, Cork. On the 14th February, 1975 I went on duty to Youghal, Co. Cork accompanied by D/Gda Ward. Later I joined two other detectives D/Gda Murphy and D/Gda McNulty in the search of a house occupied by Thomas Myers at Cork Hill, Youghal. On arrival at the house I took up a position in a laneway adjacent to the house. I jumped on a high wall at the end of the terrace and I saw three men running in the other direction away from Myers' house. They were some distance away and I called on them to "stop", saying I was a garda. They hesitated for a moment, looking back at me and then they continued towards the wall on the far side of the field. I pursued them and as I climbed over the wall I met a barrage of stones and rocks thrown by the three men. I drew my gun from its holster and called on them to stop and stand still. I succeeded in putting the three against a wall and I made a quick search for weapons. I recognised two of the men as Martin Ferris, Churchill, Tralee, Co. Kerry and Danny O'Sullivan, Barrow, Ardfert, Co. Kerry. Martin Ferris recognised me and said that he was going to walk away and that I would have to shoot him in the back. The three men then ran away and I followed and caught a man I now know to be Robert McNamara from Limerick.

As I did so, the two others turned back and then the three tried to disarm me. I resisted, broke away from them and held them at gunpoint until I received help from the other Gardaí. I then conveyed Ferris, O'Sullivan and McNamara to Youghal Garda Station in a waiting car. Later I heard Inspector Murray of the Garda Síochána formally arrest the three men under Section 30 of the Offences Against the State Act, 1939.

The transcript of Detective O'Sullivan's statement in evidence to the court tells its own story. What it doesn't say, though, is that Martin Ferris and Detective O'Sullivan were childhood friends from Churchill/Chapeltown, having been reared only a few hundred yards apart. They played a great deal of football together as juveniles in the Trough Field in Fenit. A lovely family, O'Sullivan's grandparents and parents lived in the two adjoining houses to Mary Joe Daly's grocery shop at Chapeltown, where, as related earlier, the Ferris family did most of their shopping.

The saying that Ireland is a small place is well portrayed in this scenario as three schoolfriends find themselves in such an ironically confrontational situation on both sides of the law. Detective Garda J.P. O'Sullivan, although no relation of Danny's, found himself having to make the choice of whether he would shoot two of his former childhood pals from Churchill/Barrow, in order to perform his duty as an officer of the law. Luckily he kept a cool head and took the right decision.

Ferris was interrogated for four days in Union Quay Garda Station, Cork, by Detective Garda Christopher Godkin. Ferris understood that the detective had a job to do and that he was entitled to be enthusiastic about doing it well. However, this was one of the toughest interrogations to which he was ever subjected.

On the Sunday night during a break of two hour, Ferris was placed together with Danny O'Sullivan and Bobby McNamara in the same cell for the first time since being arrested. They were all glad to see each other. They were more than surprised when a garda sergeant with a footballing background took pity on the three lads and arrived to them with three bottles of stout. As can be imagined, this gesture brought great relief to the three prisoners. Ferris, to this day, contends that this was the most welcome bottle of stout he ever drank.

On the Monday morning, after a long night of interrogation, Ferris was brought, together with McNamara and O'Sullivan, to be charged at the Cork District Court on various serious counts.

He faced a fourth heavy day of interrogation on the day after the court. His brother Brian was allowed to see him in Cork. Brian's encouragement helped: "Don't break, don't break, you'll beat them," he exhorted Martin.

In evidence, the court heard that the trio had been given a lift in her car by seven-months-pregnant Anne Gough. She and her husband Tom, a hospitable young couple, offered them accommodation until such time as the trawler they said they were expecting arrived in Helvick. As a result, former Waterford and Munster Gaelic footballer Tom Gough became a target for much interrogation by gardaí for years afterwards. The baby born to Anne and Tom Gough two months later is now Donncadha, who is a well-known musician. The three volunteers also stayed, uninvited, for a number of weeks in the empty house of international ballad singer Liam Clancy, who was in the USA at the time.

The case was eventually switched to the Special Criminal Court, and each defendant represented himself in the proceedings. Under heavy interrogation, the quietly spoken and ever loyal Danny had involved himself in both the Tralee Post Office and the Dungarvan Central Creameries raids. He dealt with his own presence only, without implicating his school pal from Barrow or Bobby McNamara. Danny O'Sullivan was convicted of the Tralee GPO and Dungarvan robberies and was sentenced to six and eight years concurrently. The gardaí believed Ferris had been present at both raids, but interrogation didn't produce the positive outcome they required or desired. Ferris was acquitted on both charges after a week-long hearing in Dublin. However, he was remanded to Portlaoise Prison pending further charges of IRA membership.

CHAPTER THREE

ACCORDING TO REPUBLICANS who endured the harsh penal system of Portlaoise Prison, the years 1975–77 were the toughest and most inhumane. Some prisoners, such as Dublin Volunteer Colm Ó Daltún and Pat Ward from Donegal, died in later years as a direct result of hunger strikes. Many hunger strikers never recovered full health and others died later.

Martin Ferris arrived in Portlaoise for the first time in February 1975, shortly after a hunger strike had ended. Conditions in the prison were bad but were to get much, much worse.

As he was being escorted to his cell after being officially admitted, his former active service comrade Brendan O'Doherty from Currow, County Kerry, was the first man he met on the bridge of E3 IRA landing in Portlaoise. They shook hands and hugged each other. They served some years together in Portlaiose as close friends, but O'Doherty's nervous system was apparently shattered. He completed an eight-year sentence, although he suffered a number of nervous breakdowns. Martin believes that the attention and kindness of Danny O'Sullivan and senior IRA Volunteer Kevin Mallon brought Brendan through his ordeal during those bad periods in Portlaoise. In fact, by 1977, Brendan actually endured an incredible forty-seven days of hunger strike. He was released in 1981 and died tragically at home in June 1984.

Martin Ferris gave the oration at his graveside. "Brendan was only in his thirties when he died, and he was a great friend of mine both outside and inside of prison."

Martin believes that Brendan's case symbolises the deprivation of medical help in prison, help which might have saved his life. That was the norm in Portlaoise under Governor O'Reilly.

During his years in prison, Martin and his friend Danny O'Sullivan would speak a lot about life in their home parish. They shared the same simple interests of the land and sea of home. As school pals from childhood, both knew and understood all of those things and knew all of the people of Barrow. With their other great friend, Brendan O'Doherty, the three would walk and talk their way for hours around the exercise yard. O'Doherty came from a farming background too, and so the three of them would discuss the seasonal changes in the farming year going on outside the high, cold stone walls of prison life. Brendan had a deep interest in the outdoor life of hunting and shooting and river fishing. Martin was with Danny in Portlaoise for a total of almost three years, although, in fact, Danny and Martin were to attempt an escape at their very first opportunity.

Ferris affirms the theory that the duty of any prisoner is to be constantly trying to buck the system and to be always seeking to escape. Others do not agree. Veteran Kerry republican Dan Keating, now a centenarian and veteran of most IRA campaigns of the twentieth century, spent seven years in various jails during his lifetime. He had a different philosophical approach from that of

Martin Ferris. Dan was willing to put down each day as it came. Ferris wanted to get out of jail each day that he spent there. Keating accepted his lot. Ferris abhorred his lot. Keating said that so many different prisoners reacted in various ways. In the forties, Jack Brady was interned with Keating in Tintown Camp, the Curragh. Keating said that every day that Brady spent in jail was like a month. He hated being incarcerated.

One day he said to Kerry republican Johnny O'Connor: "I can't understand the attitude of those four there," pointing at Keating, Mick McCarthy, Ned Carrigan and Charlie Dolan. "Dan and those three meet there every day and talk and walk, and just seem so contented in jail."

"Ah," said Johnny, humorously, "sure those four have spent so much time in jail it's the only place they ever remember. They don't know any better."[1]

Many other prisoners were not as philosophical as Dan and were continuously, impatiently straining at the leash to get their freedom. From the first minute the nature- and freedom-loving Ferris heard doors being locked behind him when entering Portlaoise, he vowed to do all in his power to try to escape. He didn't have to wait long to discover that plans were already being hatched for a major breakout by the Provisional IRA prisoners in Portlaoise.

After the ending of the hunger strike in February 1975, IRA prisoners in Portlaoise turned their energies and imaginations toward resuming an active role in the war. The prison escape attempt was being planned. Kevin Mallon, a highly respected active service IRA leader from Coalisland, County Tyrone, had been recaptured in January. At the time of his arrest, the IRA leadership were involved in delicate negotiations with British representatives aimed at finding a just and lasting solution to the conflict in the Six Counties. Shortly before his arrest, Mallon, along with Dáithí Ó Conaill, Seamus Twomey, J.B. O'Hagan and Ruairí Ó Brádaigh, had been involved in the sensitive Feakle talks with leading Protestant clergymen. The IRA had called a ceasefire and were honouring it. Great hopes and expectations were held that peace might finally be achieved. The arrest of Mallon at such a sensitive time called into question the sincerity and commitment of the Twenty-Six County government in the pursuit of peace. This was exemplified in the following months with the arrests of Dáithí Ó Conaill and J.B. O'Hagan.

With Mallon returned to Portlaoise, security in the prison was placed on high alert. So paranoid were Governor O'Reilly and his security people that they delegated a particular officer to shadow Mallon wherever he went in the prison. He was under intensive and constant surveillance twenty-four hours a day. This was over and above the usual security surveillance carried out in the prison, which was considerable in itself. The state of alert was further intensified shortly after that with the discovery of explosives on Peter Lynch, an IRA prisoner from County Derry, after a visit. Rita O'Hare, who had been visiting Peter Lynch at the time, was arrested as she left the prison. She was subsequently charged and convicted of possessing explosives in the prison and served three years as a republican prisoner in Limerick Prison. This incident happened at the end of February 1975, a few weeks after the hunger strike concluded.

As a reprisal, the prison authorities suspended all visits initially. They followed this up by putting an end to "open visits", and in their place a closed visiting procedure was implemented. This entailed a new visiting box resembling a cage. From a table which separated prisoner and visitor, two wire grilles approximately two feet apart ran to the ceiling. On the inside of both grilles were sheets of perspex rising approximately eighteen inches from the table top. An officer was seated in a cage at the end of the table only feet away from the visitor and prisoner. With a clear view of the divide between both, he was strategically positioned to enable him to monitor all conversations and take notes of these. No contact whatsoever was possible between prisoners and visitors. Both prisoners and their families were forced to endure the agony of meeting their loved ones in these conditions for the next ten years. In many cases men were to complete their sentences without ever touching their children.

After the discovery of the explosives, security within the prison was tightened further. The prison authorities believed at the time that they had foiled an imminent escape, but within two weeks the fallacy of this belief was dramatically exposed.

On St Patrick's night 1975, the IRA attempted a mass breakout from the prison. A dumper truck had been fitted with armoured plates and strengthened sufficiently to enable it to drive through one of the side gates to the prison farm. The truck had a compartment, also armour plated, which was capable of holding twenty men. Remand prisoner Ferris was to be amongst them.

Although the odds were stacked against them, Ferris firmly believes:

> Taking the opportunity to escape from a top security prison, where heavily armed soldiers are strategically placed on all vantage points, is fraught with risks. But it is not only freedom that is at stake. The very lives of the prisoners are on the line too. Apart from good planning and attention to detail, one of the other major factors favouring prisoners on an escape attempt is the element of surprise. We had that advantage. However, after that luck plays a considerable part. Volunteers of the IRA felt duty-bound to escape from prison and resume an active role in the struggle. However, it should be pointed out that all of those who took part in such an operation did so voluntarily. They had the option to decline the offer of a place on the escape if they so wished.

The escape attempt got under way in the recreation hall just after 8 p.m. There were between seventy and eighty prisoners in the hall watching a film at the time. Most of them were aware of the plan to escape and intended taking part in it. The escape attempt was set in motion when the electricity to the prison and the surrounding area was cut off. An explosive charge placed on the door leading to the exercise yard was detonated and demolished the door. Kevin Mallon and Brian Keenan led the escape; Martin Ferris was in the advance group of twenty volunteers who emerged at speed from the smoke-filled exit of the recreation hall and made their way to the south-east end of the exercise yard where their way was blocked by another gate.

By now the soldiers who had taken up their positions on the prison walls and roof lost no time and commenced firing from all angles at the prisoners. Martin recalls the scene vividly:

> I crouched with seventeen others, while two of our comrades placed explosives as we tried to blow the gate. Brian Keenan was shot in the hand and leg; the charge went off and the gates burst open. We dashed outside the door and took cover against the pumphouse wall. Other prisoners dashed down the exercise yard. The place was alive with bullets. I saw Jap Murphy being wounded badly in the leg. He stumbled and stumbled badly, and two of our comrades got up and dragged him to cover. We heard outside the wall the truck, armour-plated, in the distance, but the sound of the lorry was dying; then there was no sound. Something had gone wrong. All they had to do was hit the gates and we were out. I know now what went wrong. The engine overheated and she ceased, only twenty feet from the wall, only twenty feet from the big double doors that she had just to touch and we were out.

Having identified where the prisoners had emerged from, the soldiers in the posts on either end of the yard now also directed their fire towards the recreation hall exit.

The pumphouse gable offered some cover from the soldiers firing from the roof. However, it was completely exposed to fire from the soldiers in the security posts on the prison walls. Since the prisoners were unarmed, there was no question of fire being returned. In any case, the prisoners were forbidden from engaging the forces of the Twenty-Six County state by the IRA's General Army Order No. 8. The soldiers were well aware of this. Even in the heat of the moment, the soldiers knew they were not under fire or in any danger. It should have been obvious to them that apart from the two explosive charges the escaping prisoners were totally unarmed.

With the reality of the failure of the escape bid eventually dawning on the soldiers, the gunfire finally ceased. Confusion reigned at this stage, and the prisoners were totally unaware that one of them, Volunteer Tom Smith, had been shot dead. It was too early for anyone to piece together the entire picture. For many there was a sense of relief and almost disbelief that they had survived the hail of gunfire unscathed. Turning their attention to those around them, the uninjured prisoners found that others were not so lucky. Initially, once the checking of their comrades began, they found that miraculously only five prisoners had suffered gunshot wounds. It was evident that immediate hospitalisation was required for two of the wounded: Jap Murphy from South Armagh and Brian Keenan from Belfast. The prison authorities, it seemed, were in no rush to provide the necessary treatment. With no treatment forthcoming, the concern of the prisoners turned to anger, and they began shouting vociferously for medical attention for the wounded. In particular, they vented their frustration verbally on the soldiers. With their nerves on edge and unsure of what to do, one of the soldiers panicked and opened fire indiscriminately, putting the lives of his own colleagues as much at risk as those of the prisoners.

Fortunately for all concerned, nobody else was injured.

Chapter Three

Without regard for his own safety, J.B. O'Hagan, who had previously escaped from Mountjoy Prison, approached the army officer in charge.

> J.B. O'Hagan, God love him, at fifty-three years of age, was one of the greatest republicans I have ever known. A man who would have played an All-Ireland Final in 1953 for Armagh against Kerry were it not for being on the run. And being a full-time IRA activist.
>
> He covered Jap's badly bleeding thigh and then turned and walked towards the Free State army officer with his hands raised and shouting, "Get help quickly, there is a man badly wounded. He is bleeding to death." The officer pulled a Browning and emptied the magazine into the ground in front of J.B., who kept walking towards the officer and shouting to get help. J.B. was within touching distance of the officer. "Get a fucking ambulance quickly."
>
> Brian Keenan, wounded in the hand and leg, was still buzzing around the place trying to see is there any other way out of here.

O'Hagan successfully impressed on the army officer the urgent need for transport to be provided to take Murphy and Keenan to the hospital for treatment. The other three wounded prisoners were treated later in the prison. Two of them had been grazed in the head by bullets and the third, Martin's close friend Bobby McNamara, had a slight hand wound.

It was only when they were returning to the prison from the exercise yard, having to retrace their escape route, that the prisoners became aware that Tom Smith had been shot dead. His body lay approximately fifteen feet outside the doorway of the recreation hall. A shadow from fixed seating attached alongside the wall of the building had hidden Tom's body from view up until then, and many of the prisoners had passed by without seeing him. Apparently the body of the dead volunteer lay covered with a blanket placed on him some time earlier by an officer. It was Volunteer Donal de Barra who eventually made the sad discovery.

Ferris firmly believes that:

> Had Donal de Barra not discovered Tom's body, it is unlikely the prisoners would have been told that night that their comrade was dead. The officers probably assumed there would be a violent reaction to such news and therefore said nothing. This was perhaps understandable considering the tension, fear and anger which pervaded the prison both during and after the events surrounding the escape attempt.
>
> Tom Smith's comrades reacted in a dignified and respectful manner. His body was carried by his comrades into the prison where he was laid upon a makeshift stretcher. All 140 prisoners assembled on E1 landing where the IRA OC Eamonn O'Doherty directed the formation of a guard of honour. Two lines of IRA volunteers stretched the length of the landing and came to attention for two minutes' silence. An eerie silence descended like a dark cloud on the prison. The prisoners then saluted their fallen comrade, each man saying his last silent farewell to a friend and comrade they had been proud to know and had the privilege to serve with. A local priest then arrived and administered the last rites, and a decade of the rosary was said. A few minutes after this, it was time for Tom's body to be removed. Now only the echoes of the slow-marching falling footsteps could be heard as Tom Smith's body was solemnly borne by four of his comrades to the prison surgery. This was the last we would see of our comrade.

The night's events were not over yet, however. A short time afterwards, all the prisoners were confined to their individual cells. Extra gardaí and officers had been drafted into the prison and a major search of the prison followed. It was to last for most of the remainder of that night. Every cell was thoroughly searched and every prisoner was forcibly strip-searched. Outnumbered by six to one and sometimes more, all of the prisoners resisted the strip searches as best they could. Many prisoners suffered heavy treatment at the hands of those conducting the searches. Martin recalls:

> Gardaí and screws swept through the prison as if on a brutal and vicious spree. No one and nothing was spared as the forces of the state exacted their revenge and pound of flesh from the prisoners who had dared to challenge the right of the state to incarcerate them. Everything moveable within the cells was apparently removed, and once again republican prisoners were left sleeping on the floor. Yet despite the massive search, nothing was found.

The day following Tom Smith's killing an autopsy was carried out. No independent doctor or pathologist was allowed. Some time later an inquest was held. The findings of the inquest suggested that Tom Smith died as a result of being struck by a ricochet bullet. It further stated that it could not be determined conclusively if the bullet was fired by the army personnel on guard in the prison. Republican prisoners refuted the findings of the inquest on a number of grounds. First of all, they pointed out that the only shooting on the night in question was done by the soldiers on duty within the prison. The fact that no weapons or spent cartridges were found, other than those which came from those same army weapons, further substantiated the prisoners' claims. Nor did the inquest call any of the prisoners who witnessed the events of that night. Those prisoners were adamant, following their own investigation, that the fatal shot came from the north-east corner post. They further pointed out that fire was directed at the door of the recreation hall after the advance group of prisoners had run out, perhaps to prevent others coming through the door.

In their own inquiry, the prisoners tried to establish what exactly had happened and when it had happened on the night in question. The sequence of events they pieced together established that Tom Smith was one of the last prisoners to run from the recreation hall into the exercise yard. When he reached the corner of the recreation hall, the intensity of the fire from the soldiers on the prison roof prevented him from going any further. It is assumed that at this point, in order to take cover, he turned back towards the recreation hall door. In all probability Tom Smith ran into the line of fire and was cut down at this particular stage. He had been shot right through the forehead. Some of the prisoners who had previously seen similar wounds inflicted on people in the Six Counties maintained that that type of wound was consistent with a direct and clean shot. This cast doubt on the theory of a ricochet which the inquest thought was the likely cause of death.

Eight years later, a former soldier who had been on duty in the prison that St Patrick's night made contact with a well-known Cork republican, himself a former soldier. This ex-soldier claimed to have been present in Portlaoise Prison on the night Tom Smith was shot. He also stated that he was the sole occupant of the north-east corner post and that it was he who had shot Tom Smith. This man claimed that he directed his fire across and over the recreation hall door exit in an attempt to prevent other prisoners coming through it. He was at pains to stress that he had not fired deliberately to kill anyone. During this conversation, the ex-soldier expressed deep regret that his actions had led to the death of Tom Smith. Shortly after the Portlaoise shooting, he left the army and went to live on the Continent for a time before returning to Ireland again in the late 1970s.

Remembering this incident clearly, Martin states: "While we may accept the veracity of the ex-soldier's account, his sincerity, genuine regret and courage in coming forward, this does not in any way exonerate the actions in general of the army personnel on duty that night and their officers in particular, nor the ineffective investigation which followed. "

Hundreds of rounds were discharged into the exercise yard that night, and those who fired must have known this type of concentrated fire would prove lethal. The prisoners could consider themselves fortunate under the circumstances that casualties were not heavier.

Media reports on the events surrounding the St Patrick's night escape attempt were wildly inaccurate, and indeed distorted. Journalists and reporters appeared to unquestioningly accept the official accounts of what transpired that night. Official government sources claimed that soldiers on duty at the prison came under fire from unidentified gunmen in the fields outside the prison. Up to eighty rounds were alleged to have been fired at the soldiers. At the subsequent trial in the Special Court in Dublin of the occupants of the armoured truck, Gerry Quinn and Eamon O'Sullivan, evidence was given to this effect. However, under cross-examination this concocted story was exposed as false when state witnesses were unable to produce any physical evidence to substantiate their claims.

Martin Ferris asserts:

> Yet despite these facts, the media believed and ran with the initial distorted claims that the prison was attacked by imaginary gunmen. In fact the only assistance the escaping prisoners had came in the form of the armoured dumper truck, the cutting of the electricity to the area and vehicles parked in the vicinity of the prison to aid the prisoners' flight from the area.

A number of roads were also blocked to hinder state forces in any follow-up search which would have been set in train. We can only conclude that the circulation of such misleading information was designed to create the false impression that the IRA might have inadvertently shot Tom Smith themselves.

Ferris concludes: "It may also have been the government's intention to suppress the truth in an effort to justify the inexcusable response of its soldiers in shooting to kill prisoners who were obviously unarmed."

The official government account issued following the attempted escape and shooting dead of Volunteer Tom Smith in 1975 was remarkably similar to the government account of another shooting in Portlaoise some fifty-three years previously. This occurred in 1922 when Free State soldiers shot and fatally wounded Dublin republican prisoner Patrick Hickey in the same prison exercise yard following an attempt by the prisoners to burn the prison. Kerry veteran republican Dan Keating, now aged 103 years, was involved that day in 1922. He said, "The shooting of unarmed prisoners was as much an atrocity in 1975 as it was in 1922."

The media never once questioned why no spent cartridges were found in the subsequent searches of the immediate area around the prison. Or indeed how the government failed to provide one shred of evidence or one credible witness to verify their account of events that night. The subjective and one-sided media reports tended to concentrate on portraying the escape bid as a desperate attempt by ruthless and violent men to effect an escape, heedless of the dangers to their own lives or those of their jailers.

Ferris vehemently contradicts this :

> In fact, nothing could have been further from the truth. Notwithstanding the obvious risks involved, no effort was spared to ensure, as far as possible, that the safety of prisoners, officers and even soldiers was not jeopardised. The IRA maintains that time spent minimising the risks to life is an essential element in any IRA operation, other than those specifically targeted at the Crown forces. However, one understands

the awkward situation in which crime and political reporters find themselves. Crime and political reporters are often compromised by their sources. It is the nature of their job.

Regarding that escape attempt on St Patrick's night, Martin points to the fact that not one officer, garda or soldier was injured during their operation as evidence of the care taken by them. He stresses: "The objective of the operation was to effect the escape of the prisoners, no more, no less. The only injuries to state forces that night occurred when two gardaí batoned a screw in panic as they tried to get from the recreation hall to the main prison block when the escape attempt began."

CHAPTER FOUR

ARTIN FERRIS WAS released from Portlaoise on 14
November 1975 after serving nine months of his
twelve-month sentence for IRA membership.
He returned to his mother's house in Churchill and
immersed himself in oyster fishing and its attendant problems in the Tralee Bay oyster bed. It was wintertime and
there was little football action. His stay was to be brief; the
Special Branch surveillance was seldom far away, and a
seemingly certain wish to put Ferris behind bars again
would soon be fulfilled. His next arrest was only months
away.

Times became dangerously tough in the so-called Oyster
War, as some outside boats flouted the agreed rules introduced to protect the oyster stocks. Strikes and agreed temporary closure of the Tralee Bay bed were peaceful actions
introduced by the concerned fishermen's association, but
these had little effect on some greedy boatmen.

In the oyster season of 1975–76, the headlines in *The
Kerryman* were constantly dominated by accounts of

trouble on Tralee Bay. There was suspicion that the fishermen from outside the immediate bay area were not keeping the rules. The cardinal sin was the taking of small oysters. The lower size limit was a three-inch oyster. Anything smaller, which could pass through the ring measurement, would be in contravention of the rules. Taking small oysters would certainly harm the future harvests.

The Kerry Board of Fishery Conservators were actively patrolling the bed, and many unscrupulous fishermen from outside the area were caught red-handed in possession of the smaller oysters. A protest strike by the local fishermen was called in November 1975, and outside fishermen from Dingle and Cromane were told that they were not welcome on Tralee Bay. Ferris was involved in organising the pickets for Fenit, Kilfenora, the Spa and Derrymore across the bay. *The Kerryman* roared headlines like "No Outsiders" or "Tralee Bay Fishing at a Standstill". On 28 November 1975, the banner headline was "Oyster Boycott Continues".

Ferris was at the forefront of the drive for conservation of the bed. Limiting the size of the catch and the size of the oysters permitted to be caught were two leading points being demanded by locals. The hours of fishing and the size of trawler being used were also serious points of dissension.

While all of this was going on, the Special Branch in Kerry raided Martin's home many times. In early January 1976, he and a volunteer, Eamonn O'Sullivan, who had escaped from the Curragh Military Hospital in the summer of 1975, were driving through Naas in a white Volkswagen and were spotted by the Special Branch. The two IRA men tried to outrace the Branch and made for Athy, where they left the car and got to a safe house owned by veteran republican Frank Driver. O'Sullivan made safe his getaway, and as Ferris believed the gardaí had nothing against him at that particular time, he later returned to collect the car. Unfortunately, O'Sullivan's fingerprints were on the car, and this implicated Martin with a wanted man. His friend Jim O'Shea was arrested on 8 February and was charged with possession of a handgun. Martin's mother's house was raided ten times over the following weekend. On one raid Martin was in the house, and in order to hide him, his mother pretended to be ill in bed and hid him under the eiderdown beside her. He had taken out the light bulb so that the Branch just looked in from the door and respected her privacy.

Shortly afterwards, Frank Stagg died on hunger strike in England in February 1976. Martin attended his funeral in Mayo. On 14 February, twelve months to the day since his last arrest (St Valentine's Day was not lucky for the Kerryman), he was arrested at a roadblock in Ballinrobe. He was taken to Claremorris for questioning. On 16 February he was charged with IRA membership at the Special Criminal Court in Dublin, and three months after his release from prison, Martin was back in Portlaoise again on remand. He was convicted on 18 May at the Special Criminal Court and sentenced to eighteen months in jail for membership of the IRA.

CHAPTER FIVE

IN PORTLAOISE PRISON again, Martin Ferris found that conditions had further deteriorated over the time he had been free.

Really it was the beginning of probably one of the worst periods that I certainly and scores of others encountered in Portlaoise Prison. For a number of months, it became apparent that there was a change of engagement between the management of Portlaoise Prison, under Governor Willie O'Reilly, and the political prisoners. On 15 July an escape attempt had been made from Green Street Courthouse in Dublin, involving Jim Monaghan, Joe Reilly (Sinn Féin councillor, Navan), Dan Murphy (also from Navan) and Mickey O'Rourke. They attempted to blow their way to freedom. They succeeded in doing that, but in the follow-up searches (the place was cordoned immediately), both Joe Reilly and Jim Monaghan were arrested in nearby streets, and Dan Murphy was arrested trying to get out of the courthouse, but Mickey O'Rourke, being from Dublin and knowing the place like the back of his hand, made good his escape. That took place sometime in the late morning of that July day. Anyway, that evening the three were brought back to the prison, after being taken to the Bridewell and interrogated.

At lock-up time at half eight, it became apparent that something was going to happen, because there were extra gardaí and extra prison officers on the landings. They selected two cells, mine being one, and I think the cell of a McArdle lad from Louth. My cell was on B2 at the time, and next cell to me was big Bobby McNamara from Limerick. Immediately after lock-up, the door opened and I think about half a dozen screws came into the cell and they took out every item of furniture; that included the bed, the table, everything – nothing was left in the cell except the four walls and myself. And they asked me to strip-search, and I said, "No, I am not strip-searching." And I put my back into a corner and stayed firm. They proceeded to try and take the clothes off. I pushed them away and we got into a wrestling match. I was lying on the ground. I was hanging on to the pipe which runs right through the whole of one side of the wing as it feeds the cells. I wrapped my leg as best I could around it and held on, and they tried to pull me off it and take my clothes off. And while this was going on it was obviously very loud, and there was a lot of vibration from the pipe which travelled through that entire side of the landing. And other POWs began beating the doors, and next thing the whole jail started beating the doors. And this could be heard quite clearly outside the prison in Portlaoise town.

Anyway, the engagement between the prison officers and me got more violent, particularly as they were intent on searching me and this entailed forcibly taking my clothes off. Eventually, during a very bad encounter, I was being held in a headlock, and there were others trying to unbuckle the belt of my pants. The top I was wearing had been ripped clean off, and they were still having great difficulty in ripping my pants and underclothes off me. At one stage they were holding me around the neck, and this was going on for maybe seven or eight minutes and all they had off me was my shoes and my top, nothing else. They had me in a headlock and I was half choking. So the only way I could release myself was by biting into a hand that was choking me. There was a finger and I bit into it, and that prison officer released my head immediately. That broke the grip momentarily, but then all hell broke loose, and they tore every bit of clothing off me in a fury. I got a number of blows from batons. I had been kicked and punched, but they tore the pants clear into ribbons – a pair of navy jeans, I remember. Then I was left totally naked on the floor of the cell. I was hurting pretty badly. They went out and they threw a mattress and a couple of blankets and a pillow back into the cell and left the rest of my belongings outside the door.

I wasn't able to stand. I dragged myself over and lay on the mattress alongside the pipe, and the banging by the other prisoners continued. I think a prisoner by the name of Quinn broke out the door up on the 3s or 4s, but it continued for maybe ten to fifteen minutes before the screws finally withdrew from the landing and, obviously, went home.

Bobby Mac was beating the wall outside, and he asked was I okay, and I dragged myself over to the corner alongside the pipe and I spoke to him. He shouted to see if he could get help from one of the better prison officers. He banged on the door continuously, but there was no medical help forthcoming. So for the whole night I lay there. I spoke to Bobby on the pipe for quite some time.

I eventually fell asleep, and the next morning I heard the door open, and straightaway Bobby and Danny O'Sullivan and a few other prisoners came in, and I think it was obvious to them that I was in quite a mess. I had a pile of bruising on my body. A lot of them would have been pinch marks, kick marks and certainly baton marks. My legs were sore where they had been kicked and struck with the batons. I was badly swollen on both sides of the face. It was the first bad beating I had received in Portlaoise, and it sticks out and will always stick out in my memory. I am aware that when the prison officers were going out – the six officers or more – that one of them was bleeding from the finger where I had bitten him. I am certain that I would have at least lost consciousness or choked had I not bitten his finger, because the grip that they had on me around the neck was choking me.

Republican prisoners began twelve months of what can only be described as systematic and institutionalised mental and physical torture. It was to be a period of imprisonment in the Twenty-Six Counties that had no parallel in this phase of the struggle.

"The political and prison administration plumbed depths of inhumanity and levels of brutality that shocked even those veterans who thought they had seen and experienced it all before," Martin remembers.

What the prisoners went through during this period would be indelibly burned into their memories. A number succumbed to ill-health, depression and even suicide as a result of the treatment they had undergone. The free hand that Governor O'Reilly was given to run and control the prison as he saw fit became a mailed fist. He created and directed a regime that would try to terrorise and break the prisoners in an effort to destroy the IRA structures within the prison.

Governor O'Reilly, along with his senior staff and

selected individuals at lower levels in the prison service, set about the task in a calculated and systematic manner. "They were as thorough as they were cruel. If they didn't visit violence on the prisoners directly, they tried to get at them through mistreating and victimising their families and visitors," Martin recounts.

Martin stresses that the republican prisoners were under no illusions as to what the prison regime's objectives were. The prisoners knew too what was at stake, not only for themselves in terms of prison conditions and political status, but in terms of the wider struggle. The prisoners were determined to ensure that the regime's objectives would never be realised. Up until then, cooperation between prison management and the IRA structures had ensured a disciplined and relatively smooth day-to-day running of the prison. The prisoners knew full well that without their cooperation it would not be possible to maintain order or run the prison on anything approaching "normal" lines. Governor O'Reilly and his staff believed otherwise; hence their attempt to destroy the republican unit and treat the prisoners simply as individuals.

In response to the fierce resistance by the prisoners, Governor O'Reilly and his staff set up a special group of officers to enforce and oversee the implementation of these measures.

Chief Officer Brian Stack, the highest-ranking uniformed officer, had been transferred in late 1976 to Portlaoise Prison and had rapidly risen through the ranks to become chief officer. It is no coincidence that his arrival and subsequent promotion came about during the most intense and brutal period within the prison.

According to Martin: "Whereas [another man] was a recognised bully boy and heavy, Stack, in contrast, usually directed. Stack was a particularly vindictive individual. He would never forget a previous incident, and if he took a dislike to a certain prisoner, he would wait until a suitable opportunity arose to punish the man in some way or other. He thought nothing of having officers hold a prisoner while he struck him with his baton during a strip-search."

It seems, according to prisoners, that Stack was also despised by prison officers and prisoners other than republicans.[1]

Not satisfied with their brutal actions in cell searches, the prison's Heavy Gang extended them to the landings. Prisoners in ones and twos passing these people on the landing were sure to get an elbow or a shoulder in an effort to provoke a response. They apparently also taunted individual prisoners by sometimes mentioning the contents of personal letters and so on. Nothing was too personal or sacred in their book. If it was likely to hurt or provoke a prisoner, they were only too willing to use it as another form of psychological torture.

This Heavy Gang became an élite within the Portlaoise prison service and were looked up to by many within their ranks. To be part of the Heavy Gang and display a propensity for violence earned these individuals a certain status within their violent subculture. Many of the individuals who earned their spurs in the Heavy Gang were later rewarded with promotion.

In fairness, though, it must be pointed out that not all the screws approved of the Heavy Gang's methods and conduct. Many of the screws themselves were intimidated by this Heavy Gang and deplored its actions. Unfortunately, they lacked the moral courage at the time to stand up to these thugs and denounce their activities. This can be explained, though not excused, when one considers the context. It wasn't just the Heavy Gang they had to fear, for to challenge them would effectively mean challenging the *status quo*, the system. This could mean not only intimidation and a bad working environment; it would mean being labelled a Provo lover and might ultimately mean a transfer or indeed dismissal from the job. To stand up and be counted in such circumstances would have taken a lot of courage. But, says Martin Ferris, "There wasn't a lot of courage in the prison service at the time."

> We tried to burn the prison, and this was to highlight the terrible, inhumane conditions which were by then deteriorating rapidly within the prison. We wanted to focus public attention on our plight. And the knock-on effect of that was that the entire prison got a month in solitary confinement. That meant we were locked up twenty-three hours a day. We had one hour's exercise, each one landing at a time getting exercise. And that went on for the entire month of July into August of 1976, which was one of the warmest summers I ever remember.
>
> That was the price one paid when they resisted. And it became very apparent, after the month's solitary, that we did not know what was going to happen, that free association was gone because O'Reilly withdrew it.

It was no longer possible for IRA prisoners to move freely between the three landings they occupied. Nor was it permissible to communicate verbally or otherwise with one's comrades on other landings. Any prisoner who climbed up the wire or stairs separating the landings to talk to another prisoner was put on report and was punished with loss of remission and privileges, such as visits, letters, etc.

> It was effectively breaking the chain of command of the IRA inside the prison. I was on the base and was OC of the base along with Johnny Cashin, who was adjutant on the base with me, a young lad from Belfast who was a gymnast. Then you had various OCs. You had an OC on the 2s and an adjutant, and you had the jail command on the 3s. But there was no way of communication between landings other than climbing up on layers of wire. Anybody who tried to communicate was automatically put on report, and a loss of a month's remission was the result.

The amount of exercise in the open air was also curtailed by reducing the number of prisoners allowed to exercise at any one time, so that the separate landings had to alternate their exercise periods. Their time in the exercise yard prior to these restrictions was now reduced by one third. This also applied to recreation periods indoors.

All craft workshops were closed indefinitely. Library books were limited to three books per prisoner per week. Nothing was allowed in on visits. Only one change of clothes was allowed, and these were limited to certain colours: no yellows, navy or sky blue, red, green or black garments were allowed in. Other petty restrictions were also enforced, such as a ban on putting family photographs or political posters on cell walls. Failing or forgetting to leave the dinner plate outside the door after meals also brought sanctions on the prisoners. Nor could the prisoners bang on cell doors to get the officers' attention. Beds had to be made up in a regimented way from 8:30 a.m. until lock-up at 8:30 p.m. The list of new petty prison rules now introduced seemed endless. Failure to comply would result in the loss of privileges or remission.

Sometimes the prisoners were punished collectively through the confiscation of cigarettes. When cigarettes were confiscated, they were usually returned within a week. Sometimes, however, the prisoners would only have their cigarettes back a few days when some excuse would be found to take them again. The prisoners responded to these tactics in a variety of ways. Some displayed tremendous will-power in such a pressurised environment and simply gave up cigarettes altogether rather than let their habit be used as a weapon against them. For others, until they overcame their dependency, it was a form of torture. The craving for a smoke was so great that some would even pick up cigarette butts discarded by officers and gardaí, extract the tobacco and roll their own cigarettes using newspaper if no cigarette paper was available. Other political prisoners within the prison (INLA, etc) not involved in the protests did their best to ensure that a supply of tobacco, however small, made its way to the IRA prisoners. After several months, most of the prisoners managed to quit smoking.

However, it was in the area of prison visits that Governor O'Reilly and some of his staff were at their most vindictive. Although young and resilient himself at the time, Martin could not understand why families were being victimised.

> As captured republican activists we could in some way understand the hatred of the authorities towards us. But in extending this animosity and abuse towards our visitors, families, wives and children, who were clearly uninvolved civilians, the regime plunged to the depths of inhumanity.

Anyone who associated with republican prisoners, even family members, were considered targets for harassment and abuse when visiting the prison. The closed visits already denied prisoners and their families basic human contact. Prisoners couldn't lift and hold their children or embrace their wives. Nor could they have the privacy necessary to talk about personal and family matters because of the close proximity of the officer sitting inside the wire cage monitoring the conversation and sometimes taking notes. Furthermore, the manner in which the close-knit wire at either side of the cage was erected meant that one's vision was impaired and distorted. It was difficult to look directly at visitors, and vice versa, even for short periods.

Intolerable as those visiting conditions were, Governor O'Reilly still wasn't satisfied. He now directed that two extra officers be present on a visit. One officer stood directly behind the visitor and the other directly behind the prisoner. Any mention whatsoever of the conditions within the prison, even something said in jest, prompted immediate censure from the officers and a final warning that the visit would be terminated if there was any further mention of the subject. Many visits were ended abruptly in this fashion, some within minutes of starting. One mother who had travelled from Donegal, over 200 miles, after rising at 4 a.m. that morning in order to meet the bus, had the visit with her son terminated after a few minutes because they addressed each other in the Irish language. If the prisoner objected to such intrusions by the officers, it was not unusual for him to be roughly manhandled and physically removed from the visiting box in full view of his visitors.

"The memory of prison visits in their childhood still haunts many adults today. The memory of children crying hysterically, clinging to their distraught mothers as they looked on helplessly through the wire mesh while their father was dragged away by half a dozen screws, sometimes using batons, was not uncommon. It can't have done some of the screws any good either," Martin maintains.

Not a day went by without prisoners being put on report, losing remission and being denied privileges. Anything from ignoring an officer's order to resisting strip-searches meant a prisoner was likely to be put on report.

No longer were these searches confined to stripping the prisoners of their clothes. The body search was now introduced in an attempt to humiliate the prisoners further. Having been stripped naked, the defenceless prisoner was forcibly bent over and had his anus and private parts probed and searched. The horror lingers still.

"Every night after lock-up, the tension was almost palpable as the prisoners waited for the sound of well-shod feet tramping on the tiled landing floor, a sure indication that the searches were about to begin. Whose turn would it be tonight? Until they stop outside my door, turn the key in the lock and enter and then . . . Or would they pass on to some other unfortunate comrade's cell?"

Martin says that listening to the roars and screams, the shouting and the dull thud of flailing batons and boots as another prisoner and friend underwent a search and fought back was almost as bad as getting one yourself.

"Even if they did bypass your cell that night, there was

no question of you saying to yourself, 'Thank God, no search tonight.' If you were overlooked that night, there was always the possibility of being on the list for a search the following morning. And some comrade got it anyway. Either way it was a nerve-wracking experience."

The expectation of a search the next morning made the prospect of a good and peaceful night's sleep difficult, if not impossible. In this type of situation there was absolutely no respite from the tension and fear. Nevertheless, the prisoners were determined not to submit or be cowed. They resisted and fought back fiercely. This was an assault on a number of levels. On one level there was the overarching political assault on their status as political prisoners, which underlay and provided the impetus for the physical and psychological nature of the torture. On another level, however, the very brutal nature and perverse form these assaults were taking was also an assault on the dignity of the prisoners as human beings.

Ferris reasons that by fighting back they were not simply reasserting their political credentials. Fighting back in itself was the only dignified response to such treatment, because it was one unambiguous way of saying to those who were bent on implementing it: "This is not right; it is inhuman, barbaric and totally unacceptable. It can never be accepted by those who cherish freedom and the rights of man. It must be resisted at all costs. A man without dignity is no more than a slave."

Martin was determined not to give in:

> We started protesting, and obviously because I was so angry, these issues made me more obvious in the protest, and I ended up in solitary again. I spent the next three months there. I think I got out of solitary for a few weeks. When I came back out again it was Christmas and that was okay. After Christmas it was back into solitary again for a month, then back out for a couple of days, and back in again for a month. They give you a month and leave you back out. They

then give you another month, and that went right on up to when the hunger strike began in March. Of course the start of hunger strike was also in solitary, for about the first ten days until they took me out of solitary again.

Martin adjusted to this by concentrating on trying to outwit the system. He said it was difficult but it really depended on how a person could adapt to being alone for about twenty-three hours a day. He explained that if you had access to good books it was okay, even though you didn't have a choice of what few books you got. These were chosen by the officers, some of whom would have infantile reading tastes, to say the least.

"You might get books in which you wouldn't have the slightest interest. But a lot of them, even those books, would focus your mind on something. Maybe something political or something to do with your family."

Football became a greater friend than ever:

> In my mind, I played a lot of football matches in solitary confinement, reliving a lot of matches that I had seen down the years. You'd remember many of your pleasant football occasions and maybe not such pleasant ones too. Many matches I had actually played in were replayed in my mind time and again. The most enduring battle though was the mind game going on between some of the prison officers and yourself; that would help you too. You would be trying to ensure that they would not get the better of you. You would be trying to ensure that they didn't succeed in breaking your spirit down. And that became a battle, a very tough and continuous battle.

That psychological battle would keep him going through the day. And his few minutes of exercise, more often than not, would be in the dark of the morning before the daylight – maybe at a quarter to seven. During the day there would always be noise, with doors banging and people walking about and many voices. But at this time of morning, there was total silence. It was a lonesome time in the exercise yard when you were in solitary. Martin is adamant that there was a contrived attempt to criminalise republicans.

Periods of solitary confinement varied in accordance with the seriousness Governor O'Reilly attached to a particular charge. If an officer said he was punched by a prisoner resisting a strip-search, the prisoner usually received three months solitary confinement and two weeks loss of remission. There was no appealing such a sentence, nor could a prisoner have legal representation present. In these situations the governor wielded almost total power. Charges which weren't considered all that serious might merit anything from two weeks to two months in solitary, plus loss of remission.

Once removed to the segregated area to begin solitary confinement, a prisoner was immediately strip-searched. If he resisted he was beaten. It became a vicious circle. With constant conflict and strip-searches within the solitary confinement area, some prisoners found themselves being brought before the governor when the original period of solitary was over. In many cases, a consecutive period of solitary confinement was imposed without a prisoner ever leaving the segregated area. A few prisoners spent the best part of nine months in solitary before finally being returned to the IRA landings.

Conditions for those in solitary were desperate. There was absolutely nothing in the cells but a mattress on the floor and a few blankets. The prisoner was not allowed to wear shoes inside the cell and did not have a change of clothes, except for underwear. He was deprived of visits, letters, radio, papers and writing material. All he had to distract him were his three library books per week.

Back in 1919, during the War of Independence, there was a cell built especially for IRA prisoner Patrick Fleming. The Laois republican was the personification of defiance as a prisoner. He alone caused the authorities to rethink on a number of occasions how they could construct a cell suitable to contain him. The finished product was the epitome of brutality, and Ferris spent many months in solitary in Fleming's notorious cell in the 1970s before it was dispensed with. (See Appendix.) Brutality and insulation to muffle the screams of victims in this dungeon were the central features of the design of this cell. Cells on either side of the prisoner were left vacant to enforce a silent regime and prevent any possibility of communication either verbally or by tapping the heating pipe running through each cell.

It is difficult to understand how it was both morally and practicably feasible that such breaches of humanitarianism could be tolerated in Ireland in the second half of the twentieth century. Undoubtedly, the silence of the airwaves through Section 31 of the Broadcasting Act, which outlawed republicanism, and the supine reportage of many prominent newspapers contributed to this human rights outrage.

Those POWs who continued to climb up the wire ended up in solitary. And from that up to Christmas and on into early in the New Year, we were in and out of solitary. Many of us were in and out of solitary on a regular basis, a month in, out for a week, back in for a month, out for a week. So after Christmas we started a dirty protest, slopping out our stuff on the landings, doing various things to try and disrupt the running of the prison to try and take on Willie O'Reilly and the management. We wanted conditions restored, and we also sought the restoration of the chain of command of the IRA prisoners. We wanted this recognised within the prison. And we started on the E1 (base) and, as I say, there was no actual chain of command because we started it in the E1, and E2 and E3 followed suit. And that was after a couple of days and the smell was getting quite bad. After 8.30 lock-up at night, they brought in ordinary prisoners from D block, who would be conforming prisoners from Mountjoy. These people would be serving short sentences and would be on very good behaviour. They would be prisoners qualifying for very early release, serving short sentences with part of their sentence already complete, with little choice to refuse the governor. O'Reilly decided to use these unfortunate prisoners to break the strike.

They came in and they started to clean up. So we shouted out the spyholes at them that we were protesting and that they had to back off, and they did. They came back in again a few minutes later, and the place was saturated with prison officers, and again they were told to clean up. When they began to clean up, we started banging the doors on the landing, E1 which I was on, and it spread throughout the jail, and the cleaning party of ordinary prisoners withdrew. On the next morning I was taken out before Governor O'Reilly at around 11 o'clock, and he charged me with breach of discipline, banging the doors and using threatening behaviour towards the cleaning party of non-political prisoners. For that I got a month in solitary confinement and a loss of all privileges.

I was taken down behind the gates of the solitary cells, which were quite different from the cells in the ordinary prison insofar as they were about twice as big, they were about eight feet wide and maybe sixteen feet long. There were about eight cells in that area, and when I arrived down there they were all full. I was taken down at around about 11.30 a.m. I was strip-searched immediately. I resisted and there was a lot of violence associated with it, and I was then put into a cell that I know to be Patrick Fleming's cell. It was different from the others of the solitary cells insofar as the window of the cell was built up, built up to the extent that you only had a small streak of light on the top of it. Also the heating pipe that was running through it was encased in concrete, and there was a mattress on a slab of concrete that acted as a bed. The cell was entirely different to anything I had seen before.

So I was put in there initially, and it was a terrible cell to be in because you had no way of communicating with the prisoner on either side of you. Normally to have a conversation, it meant lying on the floor and tapping the pipe. The prisoner next door would come to the pipe and you could shout, and the voice would travel in along the pipe and they shout back, and you could at least converse with each other. In this cell that was impossible. So you were absolutely and totally in complete isolation.

The prisoner was given approximately thirty minutes of exercise per day, depending on the number of prisoners in solitary at the time. This exercise period might take place as early as 6:30 a.m. At one time, because of the number of prisoners in solitary, in order to comply with the exercise regulations (prisoners had a right to one hour of exercise a day) it became necessary for the authorities to allow two prisoners to exercise at the same time. In their effort to maintain their policy of isolation, prison management tried to force the prisoners to walk at different ends of the prison exercise yard and in opposite directions. On one occasion when the prisoners refused to comply and walked together, four officers tried to drag the prisoners away from each other. This also failed miserably with Eddie Gallagher and Ferris. The prisoners suffered the loss of the exercise period for that day as a result. The following day saw a repeat of the same thing. After this for some of the men in solitary even exercise and fresh air were denied.

In protest the prisoners retaliated by refusing to remove their shoes when returning to cells after washing their eating utensils or after slopping out the contents of the chamber pot (or "po") the prisoner had in the cell. There was no in-cell sanitation in Portlaoise at that time.

Up until this, the prisoners used to remove their shoes
before entering the cell. Now the officers were put in a
position of either removing the shoes themselves, which
meant a physical confrontation, or allow the prisoners to
wear their shoes in the cell. Prison management remained
adamant that no shoes would be worn within the cell.
The officers had to remove them from the prisoners.

I refused in my cell and Eddie Gallagher did likewise
next door in his cell. So the screw closed the door,
sent for the chief officer. The chief came and ordered
us to take off our shoes. Again no! We refused to take
them off. So the prison officer in charge of the isolation wing went on his knees, ripped our shoes off and
threw them outside the door. Within minutes the
Heavy Gang burst into the cell and ordered me to
strip-search. This was our punishment for refusing to
remove our shoes. I refused and they began the strip-
search. Again when one was resisting as best one
could, there was a lot of violence attached to it. When
they finished, after about five or six minutes, the prisoner was left with torn clothes, quite humiliated and
degraded because they were forcing the prisoners to
bend over and they were forcibly spreading the
cheeks of your anus. That happened to me that morning, and it happened to everybody else who resisted
on that morning.

At half-past eight when it was all over, they
brought in our breakfast, which was cornflakes and
tea and a slice of bread. When our breakfast was finished, the cell door opened and we were to slop out,
which meant shoes had to go on again. So we put on
our shoes and went out with our toiletries. We
washed our cup and jug, brought it back to the cell
and left our shoes on. Again, the prison officer in
charge of isolation ordered us to take our shoes off
and we refused. We refused, he went out and he
locked the door. A few minutes afterward the cell

door opened. The six screws came in and began to forcibly strip-search and do all the degrading things that attended strip-searching. Naturally, there was much violence involved again.

When they were finished they go back out and lock the door. You are left lying on the floor naked, in pain and angry, and you pick up the pieces, you put on your clothes, you lay back and think what lies ahead for the rest of the day: possibly another four of these encounters before the day ends. At a quarter past twelve you hear the trolleys coming again for lunchtime. They give you in your dinner, they leave it on the floor and lock the door. You eat your dinner, you pace the cell and you lie back on the bunk for an hour or two. At a quarter to two the cell door opens, you slop out, you put on your boots or shoes, go down wash your cup, your utensils, you come back up and refuse to take off your shoes. The door closes, a few moments later the door opens, the six screws come in again, they strip-search you, again the violence, the same way as they had done earlier that morning. They finish and go out and you lay naked in your cell. That's the third time, and it's only two o'clock.

At a quarter to four they are again pushing grub into your cell, they lock the door, you eat your grub. You wait and at a quarter to five the door opens, you go out, you slop out and come back to the cell, you leave your shoes on, they come in, they take your shoes off. The door closes. A few moments later, it opens and the six come in again, and you are strip-searched again. At about six o'clock, you gesticulate a request to go to the toilet. You put on your boots, you go to the toilet and you refuse to take them off on returning. The six come in and strip you again. And again at eight o'clock, you have your tea – two sausages, a spoon of beans, two slices of bread and a

cup of tea. Then you go to the toilet and slop out and
the same thing happens again, you are stripped again.
Six times a day, and this went on for quite a consid-
. erable time.

As March 1977 approached, it became clearer as each
day passed that nothing short of a hunger strike would be
able to highlight the intolerable conditions inside the
prison. The prisoners had been hoping to avoid a hunger
strike at all costs. At this stage, however, conditions had
deteriorated to such an extent that they could no longer go
unchallenged. In addition, the levels of brutality appeared
to be rising rather than falling. No other alternative had
the potential to command a sustained focus on the issues
and at the same time produce the pressure required to have
them properly addressed. In the past, there had always
been dialogue and negotiations between the prisoners' OC
and the prison governor, even when dates had been set for
a hunger strike to begin. With such channels of communication open, there was always some chance of a resolution
to the problem. On this occasion, however, the governor's
policy was to ignore the prisoners' OC and IRA structures
within the prison, which meant that the channels of communication were effectively severed. In this type of atmosphere, confrontation was a foregone conclusion.

The situation looked hopeless, and with no prospect of
a resolution to the problem on the horizon, the prisoners
felt they had to bring the whole thing to a head once and
for all. This was the only option now open to them to protect the integrity of the republican unit, their political status and the attendant conditions.

> When one embarks on a hunger strike, effectively you
> sentence yourself to death and you hope for a
> reprieve. And that reprieve will be if conditions are
> met, or if you fail or break along the way. If you fail
> or break along the way, it can be very damaging to
> the individual, to their own self-esteem, to their own

confidence and what they stand for. In our case, conditions were so bad that to continue what we had been enduring was out of the question. Since the attempted burning of the prison and the continuing solitary confinement and the brutality associated with strip-searches, it became unbearable. There are fates worse than death, and certainly in my opinion, and from my feelings at that point in time, to go on and be destroyed by what we were enduring was unthinkable. Our only choice was to fight back and place our starving bodies against the power of the state. That was our only alternative as I saw it.

The hunger strike by Pat Ward, Colm Ó Daltún and their comrades in 1975 was still fresh in the minds of the prisoners in Portlaoise. They had finished their hunger strike in February 1975 on the understanding of a settlement with one stroke of a pen, but that settlement had been reneged upon by Governor O'Reilly. Hunger strikes as a form of prison protest are never contemplated lightly. To use one's own body as both the weapon and the battleground is something that is only considered as a last resort. So many things had to be taken into account and weighed up before the decision to embark on the hunger strike was taken. Each man had to ask himself: were conditions so intolerable that he would be willing to adopt this course of action? Could he deal with the anguish, the excruciating pain, the physical and psychological pressure it would inevitably bring to bear on not alone himself, but his family? Had he the will-power, once the fast began, to see it through to the very painful end, to die if necessary? Would he lay down his life for his principles and his comrades? Did a hunger strike have a chance of success? Questions such as these weighed heavily on the minds of the prisoners considering the option of a hunger strike. It was not an easy decision to make. Reluctantly, the prisoners answered a hushed yes to themselves to each of those questions.

Chapter Five

Martin recalls walking the yard a few days before the hunger strike was due to begin:

> It was early in the morning. It was still dark. I was still in solitary. My comrade, and friend from home, Jim O'Shea was up at the window, as he was every morning, shouting encouragement. Taking the same risks as usual. Losing remission by the day. He shouted out to me, "Monday morning, Martin, the HS is starting!" I understood. The hunger strike was about to start. "What's your position?"
>
> I say, "I'm on it!"
>
> He says, "Get word to the rest of the lads down there!"
>
> I get word to the rest of the lads that day. Eddie Gallagher says he will go on it, even though he is not part of the IRA prison unit. Micky Quinlan says he will go on it. That's the lot from the solitary lads. On the next day I tell that word to Jim when on his daily vigil to the window. The day afterwards Jim comes back to me.
>
> "This is an IRA hunger strike only. It's not to involve anybody else. We don't want any confusion."
>
> I understand. I relay the message to Eddie in the next cell to me. And the whole jail is to go on seven days' hunger strike as a support for the twenty hunger strikers.

In order to maximise the chances of a hunger strike succeeding, it is necessary to build a public awareness campaign around the issues involved and hopefully generate sympathy and support behind those taking part in the protest. Because of restrictions on visits, censorship of letters in the prison, censorship in the media outside and a generally subservient and unsympathetic press, it had not been possible to promote awareness and focus public attention on the worsening situation inside the prison. The political climate was another factor which militated against their chances of success.

An atmosphere of fear had gripped the country during the period of the Fine Gael/Labour coalition government. The introduction of a state of emergency and the Emergency Powers Bill in the middle of 1976 gave the gardaí extraordinary powers. This allowed them to hold suspects for up to seven days for interrogation before charging or releasing them. Supplementing this attack on civil liberties were the unorthodox actions of certain élite garda gangs who employed physical torture to extract confessions from suspects in custody. In addition, the right of assembly was under attack from the reactionaries in the government. This manifested itself in the proscription of the march celebrating the sixtieth anniversary of the 1916 Easter Rising in Dublin. The "ban" was ignored, and over 100,000 people took part.

Under another bill planned for introduction – the proposed Criminal Law Bill – plans were also afoot to impose almost complete censorship on the media. This was dramatically exposed when the distinguished *Washington Post* journalist Bernard Nossiter informed Tim Pat Coogan, then editor of the *Irish Press*, of the contents of an interview he had had with Conor Cruise O'Brien.[2] In this interview O'Brien produced cuttings of letters to the editor from the *Irish Press* and indicated that he intended to take action under the Criminal Law Bill against editors who published such letters. Coogan subsequently published strong editorials in which he outlined and exposed O'Brien's impending attack on the freedom of the press. In consequence, the Criminal Law Bill was undermined and diluted somewhat. What this demonstrated was that it was politically unacceptable for the press to be intimidated overtly. However, the press in general, with a few notable exceptions, did succumb to governmental pressure and turned a blind eye to abuse of power by the coalition government and state agencies such as an Garda Síochána and the prison administration. The treatment of republican prisoners in Portlaoise Prison and republicans, nationalists

Chapter Five

and civil libertarians throughout the country was all but ignored by the press. These factors taken together combined to generate a climate of fear throughout the country. Conor Cruise O'Brien, as minister for post and telegraphs, wielded considerable power over the media. He was fully supported by his colleague, the minister for justice, Paddy Cooney. Together they were the main architects of these measures. When all these factors were taken into account, the prisoners realised that whatever action they took they would be starting from the weakest possible position.

Inside the prison, the IRA prisoners discussed their position long and hard and expressed their doubts and fears. Some had serious reservations about the prospects of a hunger strike succeeding. So desperate had the situation become, however, that to allow conditions to continue as they were without confronting them as a unit would almost certainly lead to individuals taking the initiative. In any case, the prisoners knew that stepping back now would only serve to postpone the inevitable and prolong the agony of the suffering prisoners. Reluctantly, the IRA within the prison sanctioned the hunger strike. The IRA leadership outside were informed of the decision and tried in vain to persuade the prisoners to abandon this course of action.

On 6 March 1977, Martin Ferris was one of twenty IRA prisoners who began refusing food. His school pal from Barrow, Danny O'Sullivan, and Brendan O'Doherty from Currow were also amongst them, as was Bobby McNamara, who had been arrested with Ferris and O'Sullivan in Youghal. Two of the hunger strikers, Kevin Mallon and Dáithí Ó Conaill, were also designated as negotiators, with the authority to agree terms for ending the fast. Ferris believes it was a mistake to include negotiators amongst the hunger strikers. It was too much to ask them to participate while acting as representatives for the prisoners. Nelson Mandela said: "Only free men can negotiate. Prisoners cannot enter into contracts."[3]

The central demand in Portlaoise was for a public enquiry into conditions inside the prison, which, it was hoped, would lead to a general improvement. Ten days after the fast began, the governor had the twenty hunger strikers moved to one side of E1 landing. Conditions similar to those in solitary confinement were imposed. The prisoners were in breach of the prison rules by refusing food, so, technically, the governor was within his rights to isolate them. From the humanitarian point of view, one can judge O'Reilly for oneself. This was to be the first time, in this phase of the struggle, that fasting prisoners in the Twenty-Six Counties were deliberately isolated for the duration of a fast. Heretofore, fasting prisoners were allowed to stay on the republican landings at least up until such time as hospitalisation was deemed necessary. They received no letters, visits, radio, papers, cigarettes, etc.

The base, or E1 as they call it in Portlaoise, was totally segregated from the rest of the prisoners, just single cells in a line. The hunger strikers were in solitary confinement conditions again. The windows of their cells looked over and on to the exercise yard, but when the rest of the prisoners would be out in the exercise yard, about twice a day between 10.30 a.m. and 4 p.m., O'Reilly put a prison officer and a guard standing at every window so that no contact was possible, verbal or otherwise, via the cell window with the other prisoners in the yard. When the prisoners were going out and in from the yard, they were prevented from communicating with the hunger strikers in solitary by a prison officer and a guard stationed outside each of the cell doors. They were unable to give the hunger strikers any news or encouragement. It also meant a twenty-three hour lock-up for them.

Every day, meals were placed in the hunger strikers' cells as a matter of course, and food was left there for the entire twenty-four hours. The idea behind these tactics was simple: isolate the prisoners, deny them the solace, comfort and support of their comrades, and hope to gradually weaken their resolve to continue on the fast. The food, too, would be both an added temptation and the fulfilling of the authorities' responsibility to provide sustenance to those in their custody. In this case the stress was on the former, with extra portions on each plate to emphasise the point.

The first few days of the hunger strike are not too bad. I'm still in solitary for the first nine or ten days. The worst part is the food being placed in the cell at mealtimes. The most appetising food we had yet seen in prison is now being provided at mealtimes. It's bad, but otherwise one has only the isolation to battle with.

Breakfast is especially good. Either porridge or cornflakes, bread, tea and blackcurrant jam and everything you would normally like for breakfast under different conditions.

You ignore it.

At dinnertime, the untouched breakfast tray is removed. I will never forget a certain one of those days when lamb chops with onions and gravy, mashed potatoes and beautiful boiled rice as a desert sat on the tray during the afternoon until being taken out to be replaced by rashers, sausages, beans and tea in the evening meal. All trays were left there in the cell until the next mealtime. They were only taken out to be replaced by something new and fresh. Overnight they left bread and cheese in the cell. This was difficult. It never happened before.

Every morning now they got sixty minutes of exercise. The authorities obviously believed that increasing the fresh air and exercise would increase the weakening prisoner's appetite for food and lessen his resolve to carry on with the hunger strike. There was even an improvement in the variety of books for the prisoners.

The parish priest, Fr Brophy, visited every hunger striker and tried to dissuade him from the course he was on –

from a Catholic religious point of view. "To starve yourself to death was effectively to condemn oneself to hell." He used this in an effort to influence them in a very vivid way. The prisoners identified the priest's activity as another instrument of the state. They saw an absence of that concern for their souls when it came to accommodating the prisoners for Holy Communion at Sunday mass. Fr Brophy cooperated with the governor by trying to distribute the host through a wire mesh on to their tongues. Under protest he eventually gave them communion in an agreed space at a doorway.

Martin's strength was ebbing. On day 25 or 26, there was a confrontation with prison officers on a landing when Eddie Gallagher passed some packets of tobacco to Martin for his IRA comrades who smoked. The confrontation between this handful of prison officers and Martin brought Danny O'Sullivan, Brendan O'Doherty and Dáithí Ó Conaill to Martin's assistance. Martin passed the tobacco to Ó Conaill before being frogmarched into his cell. It was the day that he became aware of the deterioration of his health when it took only two prison officers to overpower and strip-search him.

> As always, I tried to resist, but I knew then that I was no match in resisting even two screws. They had an easy job in doing it. It was an awful experience. That night I had a bad reaction, with pains and empty vomiting. I felt awful, but I had felt awful the night before and the night before that. It was happening for quite a while, but on this occasion the screws tried to entice me to take sustenance of barley water or of a cup of tea. I can only assume that the mock compassion and given my weak ability to resist them physically that day was now the opportunity for them to break my determination to continue with the fast. On the offer of tea, I didn't say anything: I just looked at him with contempt and he left.

Chapter Five

As the hunger strike progressed, the men's resistance to the cold weakened. E1 landing is located on the ground floor and is one of the coldest landings in the block. It was still the month of March. A request to the governor for the hunger strikers to be moved to either E2 or E3 landings was denied. Any request that might mean easing their pain was denied. The prison doctor, while agreeing with the prisoners' request on medical grounds, was not prepared to exert his influence. Had he insisted on the move, the prisoners felt, the governor would have had no other option but to comply.

The nights were worse for the hunger strikers. "I got massive pains, vomiting, breathlessness and empty retching. This happened mostly at night; it was okay by day, but whatever it was about the night . . . We took water and salt tablets, but it was becoming more difficult to keep the water down. Empty retching and vomit water and empty retching. Not as bad during the day, but always worse at night."

A few members of the Visiting Committee who visited a couple of the hunger strikers in their cells showed little sympathy with the prisoners' plight. Their only function, it seemed to the hunger strikers, was to relay the governor's and the government's line on the fast, which was to inform the prisoners that the hunger strike would not succeed; their demands would not be met. Prison management could depend on the support of nominally independent bodies as always.

Some of the local priests did visit the hunger strikers and give them the sacraments in their cells. They expressed understanding, sympathy and concern. The priests informed the hunger strikers that the relevant authorities had been informed of their concern for the prisoners and the conditions that they had to endure. However, they were not prepared to comment publicly.

Fasting prisoners who wished to and were able to climb the stairs to attend mass in the prison chapel did so. Like those in solitary before them, however, they too were herded into the purpose-built wire cage, segregating them from their comrades.

After twenty-five days of prisoners' being on the fast, with their conditions weakening at various rates, the authorities began to transfer some of the fasting prisoners to the Curragh Military Hospital. By day 32, into the second week of April 1977, all of the hunger strikers had been transferred. Big Bobby McNamara, Gerry Quinn, Kevin Mallon and Martin Ferris were the last hunger strikers to be transferred.

> By chance I happened to be the last of the four transferred that day. It was a unique experience as I could hear the shouts of support and encouragement from the IRA prisoners on the landings above me. I was forcibly strip-searched on leaving and forcibly strip-searched on arriving at the Curragh forty minutes later, even though I had seen nobody but prison officers to whom I was handcuffed since I was strip-searched in Portlaoise.

One prisoner in particular, Kevin Mallon, because he resisted the strip-search, was handcuffed to the hospital bed in retaliation. The handcuffs were only removed when a medical orderly intervened. All this was meant as an example to the other prisoners on the fast. There would be no kid-glove treatment here, no sympathy. Security once more remained of paramount importance. However, the medical staff did treat the prisoners with kindness.

"Although we were not cooperating with them, they were brilliant, and there was a great sense of caring about them. I never experienced that in Portlaoise Prison, ever."

Outside the prison, growing concern for the plight of the prisoners was manifesting itself in public support for their demands. A mass demonstration was held in Portlaoise town in early April. The demonstrators began to converge on the prison, but 500 metres short of their destination, they found their way blocked by the garda riot squad, with heavily armed soldiers and Special Branch detectives in reserve. As the demonstrators approached the cordon, the garda riot squad swung into action and baton-charged the crowd. Those who were able fought back, and some fierce hand-to-hand fighting erupted. However, the gardaí were well equipped with batons, helmets with visors and heavy clothing. The protesters had little chance against this well-organised, well-protected and vicious force.

The crowd began to scatter in all directions as the garda onslaught continued. Anyone caught in their way was given "the timber" and bludgeoned to the ground. Neither age nor youth was considered. No one was spared. Frail old men and women got the same treatment as the youths caught by the police. Many of the protesters were injured, some with serious head wounds. One of the protesters, Sean Brosnan from Dingle – a noted fisherman and republican who was a former Sinn Féin election candidate – was in his sixties at the time and suffered head injuries as a result of being struck by a police baton.

The opinion expressed by neutral and objective observers was that the garda actions were completely over the top. Many of those who received bad beatings, it was pointed out, had been at a considerable distance from where the disturbances broke out and couldn't possibly have been involved or constituted a threat of any kind.

Further protest marches in Dublin and throughout the country passed off peacefully. In Kerry, with two local lads, Martin Ferris and Danny O'Sullivan from the Fenit, Churchill and Barrow area on hunger strike, there was a huge groundswell of support and grave concern building up. A meeting of the Churchill Cumann of Fianna Fáil was attended by sixty people who passed a unanimous motion of support for their two neighbours. A letter was sent to the secretary of the Fianna Fáil party, Seamus Brennan, stressing the concern felt and expressing their anxiety at the situation.

Public support continued to grow as people became more aware of the deplorable and inhumane conditions within the prison. Influential people of conscience began to take an active role, most notably Auxiliary Bishop of Dublin James Kavanagh, along with Senator Michael Mullen, general secretary of the Irish Transport and General Workers' Union (ITGWU), the largest trade union in Ireland. Mullen, an appointee senator of then Taoiseach Liam Cosgrave, attempted to promote negotiations. Mullen, himself a former internee and IRA volunteer in the 1940s, was acceptable to republicans as an arbitrator. The government's public position was uncompromising. There would be no concessions to the hunger strikers' demands, they said.

Censored news coverage provided some limited insight into the conditions of the now seriously ill hunger strikers. Inside the Curragh Military Hospital, the men continued to suffer greatly.

> The length of the day was enormous. Like everybody else – and I think I can speak authoritatively in this regard – the amount of sleep you got was practically nil. I can remember at all hours of the night looking across at the military police and talking to the prisoner who was next to me, who for some time was my friend Brendan O'Doherty from County Kerry. During the day you spent your time looking at the big windows and the natural light. All of that, the pains of hunger, the craving for food. Now this affected hunger strikers differently. But from the very first day until effectively one began to lose consciousness, I craved for food every moment of it. Without a doubt it was one of the most difficult things I ever had to endure in my life. Every day was a nightmare, getting from hour to hour. And that is what it was, a struggle from hour to hour, from day to day.

Prisoners found themselves dreaming of food by day and night; they hallucinated about the most delicious of dishes. Like any one of the other nineteen hunger strikers, all Martin Ferris had to do was say that it was over.

The thought of dying was constantly on my mind. Not so much the dying itself, but had I the courage and strength to see it through if needs be? And I had doubts every moment of the day. I had doubts that I could ever see it through, number one, and I kept looking for excuses to find a way to come to terms with myself if I ever came off it. And yet my senses were never as sharp as they were then. My power of recall and even my spelling, which normally is terrible, was perfect. I remembered things clearly that I had learned going to school.

Most days I felt I couldn't see it through if it came to the defining moment, and this puzzled me. I had been in situations which were fraught with danger in my life and come through them. But this was different. Why had I such doubts now? I kept trying to figure out why. And then I wondered, if I did walk away from it, how would that affect me from a psychological point of view? How it would affect my sense of being? In other words, I spent every day of that hunger strike challenging myself, challenging what I was and challenging what I had been involved in – every aspect of my life. And during that period, without having seen my mother or having met my mother for months and months, or spoken to my mother or having a letter from her or sent a letter to her or having any communication, I grew unbelievably close to my mother and my brother.

Because I was so isolated and so alone, like everybody else, I recognised and realised the enormous love she had for me as her son. The way she stood by me down through the years. The pain I had brought to her door. The continuous house raids, I being missing, not knowing where I was. The expectations she had for me that I never fulfilled or never could.

The tremendous love that she had for me. And in my moments of strength in the hunger strike and regarding the future of it, I had a feeling of the enormous pain I was inflicting on my mother and my brother. However, with the support of my comrades and the belief in our struggle, we continued.

After forty days a number of prisoners had come off the hunger strike. I appropriate no blame to them. I fully understood what they were going through at that moment in time. It didn't make them any less than me or anybody else, and their pain and their families' pain was no different than mine and everybody else's. And one must always recognise that when you are on hunger strike as we were, a split-moment decision taken by a person on hunger strike to end it, as each and everyone will tell you when it happened, twenty minutes afterwards they broke down. That's because once they were off it there was no way back. It could happen to any one of us at any moment when one felt weak and had taken a decision and then realising – oh my God, I've left my comrades behind. And I want to emphasise to my comrades who came off it that there was no sense of anger or disappointment for those who came off the strike.

It's the bond of comradeship. You had to be on it to understand it and to understand for those who came off it. I have heard comrades afterwards criticise them, but they weren't on it themselves and they wouldn't be able to understand. We understood. It is for very drastic and pressurised reasons that one takes the decision at that moment. Ten minutes later they might have taken a different decision. Some of these comrades felt they let everybody down, but they didn't; they did their best. And I always recognise in a comradely way and in an admirable way that they were committed themselves to do their best on the hunger strike, and they did.

Chapter Five

Bishop Kavanagh visited the Curragh Military Hospital and met with both Ó Conaill and Mallon on day 39 of the fast. Fr Des Wilson from Belfast was another cleric who used his good offices to secure a settlement. He had also visited the prisoners just prior to Bishop Kavanagh's visit. After forty days, two of the prisoners ended their fast, followed by four more over the next few days. After forty-five days without food, the remaining fourteen hunger strikers were finally allowed a visit.

A military policeman (MP) told Ferris he was getting a visit. One of the other lads had had a visit the day before. On roughly day 43 of the strike, they started giving visits. It was to try breaking down the strikers' will-power when they met family. Martin's mother and his brother came up to visit him sometime towards the end of April.

> Anyway, the MP came in and said my mother was outside and was I taking the visit? I said I was. Before that my mother and brother would have been given a visit only if they agreed to ask me to come off the hunger strike. But they refused to do that. So, for not cooperating with the authorities, they were deprived of a family visit. Anyway, when I was taken out to the visit I had to be taken out in a wheelchair. We could not walk much at that stage.

He was taken to a small room where there was a table with the usual wire mesh and a perspex divider, rendering impossible any contact between the prisoner and the visiting family.

> I was wheeled into the room. My mother was standing up at the wire, looking at the hopelessness of our situation through the wire partition between us, looking through the wire as I was wheeled in towards them. My brother Brian was looking at me through the wire; he too looked stunned. But the one thing that will stay with me for the rest of my life was the expression on my mother's face, the shock on her face

when she saw me. And it was only momentarily because she knew that I probably saw the shock on her face. I saw the expression of shock written all over her face, but then she changed and smiled, and I knew exactly by the shock on her face how much we had deteriorated.

For the twenty-five-year old, by now seriously emaciated, it was the worst day in his life: "It was my lowest hour. I was down to seven stone, twelve pounds from a fit twelve stone. My mother later told me all you could see of my face was teeth. I had no lips."

When mother and son met, it was the first time in a year that they had seen each other. He had been in solitary confinement for nearly six months prior to the hunger strike. Now he was a sick man in a wheelchair, looking years older than his age, and was dressed in pyjamas and a dressing gown. For the previous period before his arrest, he had been on the run and out of County Kerry, away from home. Here with a barrier of perspex between them there could be no embrace by mother and son. However, eye contact between them reassured his spirit. It was okay with herself and Brian; they were fully behind him. She didn't cry. She would save her crying for later.

"We are 100 percent behind you in your decision, whatever that decision may be. Both Brian and myself are totally behind you. We are not here to try to sway your decision in any way. We came to express our support for whatever decision you take."

With his strength ebbing away, his voice exceptionally weak and his spirits flagging, Ferris felt her support was lifting a huge weight off his shoulders, he says today. Any worries he had about his imminent death and leaving his mother and brother behind after his death were allayed by their own strength.

My mother and Brian were very brave. They put on a great act, although I realised they were going through hell. It was very difficult for all of us. As she and Brian left the Curragh Military Hospital for the long journey to Kerry on that April evening in 1977, I believed I would never see them again. But, having received their unquestionable support, I felt a great weight, worry and responsibility had been lifted. I was now resigned and ready for death with my mind at peace. There would be no turning back.

What Martin didn't know was that when his mother left, she broke down uncontrollably and wept in the arms of Sinn Féin member Marie Hoare who was waiting in the car.

Two days later the hunger strike ended, after forty-seven complete days of hunger strike and after a second visit from Bishop Kavanagh. The bishop brought a message from Michael Mullen which contained the basis for a settlement of the hunger strike. The prisoners were led to believe that the proposal for a settlement was known to and recommended by the IRA leadership outside. As related to the prisoners themselves at the time, it was said that influential people associated with the government, and in particular the opposition Fianna Fáil party, had guaranteed that once the prisoners ended their fast there would be almost immediate improvements in conditions. Bishop Kavanagh explained that he was told by Michael Mullen, who said he was in direct contact with the IRA, that in the light of what was on offer no useful purpose would be served by continuing the fast. It later transpired that no message had been sent to the fasting prisoners from the leadership. Somewhere along the line, the communication between Michael Mullen and Bishop Kavanagh was misinterpreted or misunderstood. When the prisoners ended their fast, they did so in the belief that core issues which led to the hunger strike would be addressed.

The IRA leader, Dáithí Ó Conaill, who was also on the hunger strike as a fellow prisoner in the Curragh, was wheeled to Ferris's bedside to tell him the hunger strike was over.

"I was sleeping mostly now for twenty-four hours and drifting in and out of consciousness when they wheeled Dáithí in to tell me the strike was over. And I'm told I found it hard to comprehend what he was saying. I kept saying, 'We'll keep going! We'll keep going!' "

Government statements suggested the hunger strike had been faced down and no concessions given. However, the republican prisoners were satisfied with the promises made to them and the guarantee of immediate improvements in conditions. Conditions did improve, albeit slowly. The improvements helped to ease some of the pressures in the prison. Perhaps the most significant move was the initial recognition of IRA structures within the prison, a prerequisite if any further improvements were to follow. Abolition of the infamous and degrading body searches followed shortly afterwards, though strip-searches continued. Also discontinued were some of the petty restrictions normally associated with other prisons and regimes: putting dinner plates outside cell doors, folding one's bedclothes every morning and so on. It was at this point in time that the two extra officers were withdrawn from the visits and the cage was removed from the chapel. In short, many of the more provocative sources of tension were removed.

Shortly after the new Fianna Fáil government took office, the editors of the three national daily papers were invited into the prison to view for themselves the prevailing conditions. The *Irish Press* editor, Tim Pat Coogan, in his book *The IRA*, refers to his observations at the time. He said evidence of tensions still remained. There were sixteen uniformed gardaí patrolling the floor of each landing, for example. He also mentioned reports of families left standing in all types of weather outside the prison waiting to be allowed in to visit. Often visits were denied to people after their travelling long distances. The most degrading and detested practice of strip-searching, which some prisoners endured many times in one day, was still carried out.

He also wrote that some prison officers and justice officers confided to him that, "We were pushed all the time. The objective was to ensure that the Provisionals were confronted at every hand's turn, when the familiar Republican defiance of prison regulations began."

The prisoners were now facing a long period of recuperation; for some it would take years to regain some normality to their health. For some it would never come right, and early death was inevitable.

A little thing still lives in the mind of Ferris after all the years since 1977: "When you begin to recover and to start noticing unimportant silly little aspects of life, I remember noticing that my weight made no impression on the bed. It's a silly observation, but I noticed that I was so light that my body hardly tossed the sheet on the bed."

When he was put on the scales after the strike, he had lost four stone. He said other people, heavier people, lost more weight. Lads who were sixteen stone might have finished up the strike at nine stone.

He had always been fit because he played a lot of sport. Earlier in that period in prison, he played football in the yard and did plenty of running. But for five or six months before the hunger strike, he had spent almost all of the time in solitary confinement.

> Looking back on it, were there another course of action available that would have brought to a head what was happening in Portlaoise Prison, it would have been by far more preferable to me. However, there was no option, and that was the road we went down. The end result of it was that the hunger strike ended on the 26th or 27th of April 1977, and within six weeks Paddy Cooney was no longer minister for justice, Conor Cruise O'Brien was no longer minister for post and telegraphs, Liam Cosgrave was no longer taoiseach. That coalition government was defeated and Fianna Fáil was returned to power with an unprecedented majority. In its own way, the events

of Portlaoise Prison and the brutality and viciousness associated with it contributed to bringing down that government. I have no doubt about that.

Of the twenty prisoners who embarked on the 1977 hunger strike, six have since died: Dáithí Ó Conaill (Cork), Phil O'Donnell (Derry), Mick Brody (Clare), Brendan O'Doherty (Kerry), Joe Ennis (Cavan) and Liam O'Mahony (Laois). All six died prematurely. The effects of forty-seven days on hunger strike must have contributed a great deal to their untimely deaths. The other fasting prisoners were Danny O'Sullivan and Martin Ferris (Kerry); Kevin Walsh and Bobby McNamara (Limerick); Jimmy Nolan (Tipperary); John Carroll (Offaly); Jim Ferry (Derry); Tom Bannon (Donegal); Fintan Hearty and Tommy Keenan (South Armagh); Seamus Swan (Wexford); Sean McGettigan (Monaghan); Gerry Quinn (Dublin); and Kevin Mallon (Tyrone).

Martin states: "Our initial demand on undertaking the hunger strike was for a public inquiry into the running of Portlaoise Prison. That was never granted, but maybe it's not too late yet."

CHAPTER SIX

FTER HIS SECOND period of imprisonment in
Portlaoise Prison, Martin Ferris was released on 20
June 1977, just less than two months after completing forty-seven days on hunger strike. His twenty-five-
year-old body was shattered and battered from the ordeal,
but as he walked out on to the Dublin road with his black
sack of scant personal belongings, a whole new life was
about to open up before him. He didn't know it, but his
great friend Áine Lynch was bringing his future wife to
collect him minutes later. Marie Hoare, whose parents
were both Irish, came to Ireland and settled in Ardfert. She
was reared in a very Irish republican home in Australia.
Through membership of the Sinn Féin party in Tralee, she
had become friendly with Mick Lynch's daughter Áine.
Now, things were about to radically change for Marie for
the rest of her life.

Marie recalls:

> In June 1977, I was at the Ballybunion Bachelor
> Festival with Áine Lynch on the night before Martin

Ferris was due to be released. I had got to know Áine very well within Kerry Sinn Féin. She turned to me at one stage at the festival and said: "Oh, I have to pick up Martin Ferris from Portlaoise in the morning; he is being released. Will you come up with me? I'll never stay awake without company otherwise."

So we left Ballybunion at 5 a.m. and proceeded to drive to Portlaoise to collect this Martin Ferris, whom I had never seen before. We got there and were a few minutes late. On the street outside Portlaoise Prison, I saw a man walking along with a black plastic bag over his shoulder, and I thought to myself, he looked so badly dressed, I couldn't help but noticing. His hair was very fine on his head and he was very thin, and I remember his clothes were atrocious. The jeans were up above the ankle, and he had a big black sack over his back. I said to Áine Lynch, "That's him!" and she said, "Don't be ridiculous. That's not Martin Ferris!" So she did a back look and she said, "Oh, my God, it is him!" So she pulled in and that's when I first met him – on the Dublin Road, Portlaoise – outside the prison gates. He was in terrible condition.

It took Martin many months to regain any semblance of his original strength. But he gradually began to recover his appetite for food and for football. Life returned to normal, and in September 1977 Martin and Marie moved in together.

I knew Martin was involved in the struggle. We started living together in that September, and he never ever once mentioned how seriously he was involved, but then Martin has always been the type to keep things to himself. It was only when we had a serious house raid in our home a few months later that I realised just how deeply he was involved. On that occasion he was arrested, and there was a neighbour who said the house was surrounded by Branch men with Uzis and they had taken him away down to the Barracks. I was also pulled in and questioned and was threatened that I would be deported if I got serious with him or if I intended to marry him. And it was after that that I realised that he must have been very heavily involved. I was living in Tralee at that time. That raid was about three months after I met him. I couldn't have been deported because what the Special Branch never knew was that my father took out Irish citizenship for all of us children in Australia from the time of our birth. So I am an Irish citizen! I am not an Australian citizen.

When he had asked Marie to marry him, he romantically offered his hand but unromantically insisted that she would come first before everything, except the "struggle". "The movement will come first," he said.

She was from a strong republican family herself, and her cousin Mattie Dowd had been in Portlaoise Prison with Martin in 1975. She was already a member of Sinn Féin before she met him. She accepted his proposal. They were married on 6 January 1978 at Giles Registry Office by the late Norman Chard, a fine old Orangeman in his time.

It was a fairly hectic year ahead. Football fitness slowly returned to the twenty-six-year-old Ferris, to the extent that he lined out with his club, Churchill, and was again showing signs of his original inter-county potential.

He was called into inter-county training with the great Kerry team in Killarney under the maestro, Mick O'Dwyer, for the clash with Cork in the 1978 Munster Final. It was a Kerry team destined to win four All-Irelands in a row, and then after a break in 1982 they won another three in a row – an incredible seven titles. Ferris was that close to the greatest Gaelic football team in history. But in 1978, in his state of health, he was finding the training extremely severe. Most of the Kerry players of that period will tell you they actually trained in preparation for Mick O'Dwyer's severe sessions.

Mikey Sheehy said, "You had to go into special training to be ready for Kerry team training under O'Dwyer. All of the Tralee-based players trained on Banna Beach and through the sandhills throughout the year."

Ferris's natural wild strength and stubbornness saw him through many heavy training sessions in Fitzgerald Stadium in Killarney. As with the other players, his body was wrecked from the harsh sessions. But he realised he was going to the sideline to vomit more often than the other players.

O'Dwyer was a hard taskmaster. He was never a great believer in the now customary stretching session prior to training. If training was set for 7 o'clock, then it began sharp on the appointed time. Players who wanted to do their stretching did so at 6.45. A warm-up of two laps was followed by three-quarter speed sprinting, and then the serious action continued for almost two hours of continuous running. This was the norm. Maybe a short football match and tactics capped off the session. Self-doubt about his future in the game lingered in Martin's mind. It was exceedingly difficult to do that training three or four nights a week and be involved with the IRA. And still the Kerry management considered him fit enough to be named in the squad for the Munster Final against Cork in 1978.

On the Friday before the Munster Final, the Special Branch arrested Ferris and held him in Tralee Garda Station.

"We were living in my brother's house in Caherslee, Tralee," Marie recalls.

> We were continuously raided at that stage. Martin was for ever being arrested, lifted for twenty-four hours or forty-eight hours. A great friend of ours, the famous Kerry footballer Joe Keohane, was a regular visitor to our home. Martin was training with Kerry for the Munster Final and Joe was a selector. I think that was when I turned very angry. I knew Martin had enormous football talent and because there was

an IRA action in the area, I can't remember exactly what it was but they arrested many sympathisers and republicans, but not Martin Ferris. He was in the squad with Kerry for the big game against Cork in Pairc Uí Chaoimh, Cork, on the following Sunday. So the Special Branch lifted him instead on the Friday before the game. I knew that it was so vindictive. I remember Joe Keohane going down to the garda station begging to get him out. "Look, you know the team is leaving for Cork and Martin Ferris is supposed to be travelling with them. Will you let him out, will you let him out?"

But the team travelled without him. He was kept in custody. I believe to this day that he missed his big chance of ever being on the Kerry senior team. The County Board sent Dan Ryan in a taxi to collect him on Sunday when he was released, but he was much too late then.

Well known republican Dan Ryan, an internee in the 1940s, a hackney driver from Tralee and a former Kerry and Austin Stacks' footballer, collected Martin Ferris from Tralee Garda Station three and a half hours before the throw-in for the start of the Munster Final in Cork's Pairc Uí Chaoimh. They raced to Cork, but of course Ferris was too late to get an official Kerry jersey when he arrived at the team hotel, and he was unable to be involved in the thrilling encounter. He saw Kerry beat Cork after a tough battle. They would advance to an All-Ireland Final against Dublin in which Eoin "Bomber" Liston scored a record 3–4.

Ferris ceased to remain in the Kerry training panel after the Munster Final. He found the training too severe on his overall condition of health. Medically, he was advised to desist from training at that level due to the effects of the hunger strike and solitary confinement in the previous year. It seems remarkable that he even gained sufficient form to return to club football, let alone be recalled to

Kerry inter-county football. After this Ferris faded out of inter-county football limelight.

His other passion, which was the armed struggle, would take centre stage in his life. A number of his Kerry colleagues would sail into the record books for their incredible achievements on the field of play in a Kerry jersey. But Ferris had sacrificed all of these chances of football glory at the top of the game in order to commit himself fully to his "work for Ireland's freedom".

The legendary Mikey Sheehy played and trained with Ferris in those halcyon days in Kerry football. The winner of eight senior All-Ireland medals from 1975 to 1986 said of Ferris: "He would certainly have won senior All-Ireland medals if he could have given it all of his time. He had everything a top class player needs to make the grade. Somebody of Martin's drive, strength, hands and guts would have been the ideal target man. The incomparable Eoin Liston eventually filled the bill at number 14, but Martin would have made that team in a number of positions."

By the spring of 1978, Martin Ferris would seem to have had the world at his feet. He was happily married, was mad about their son Eamon, they were expecting their first daughter Oonagh later that year, and he was training with the Kerry senior football team. What he needed now was a good fishing boat to fulfil the passion for his favourite occupation.

Early in 1978, Minister for Fisheries Brian Lenihan responded positively to an approach by me for a Department of Fisheries "grant and loan aided boat" for Martin Ferris. He looked on it very favourably, saying, "I believe in giving any good man a second chance." On 22 May of the same year, Lenihan wrote to Martin and again to me, saying he was trying to expedite the matter and that he hoped he would have everything sorted out soon. The old familiar saying of Brian's – "No Problem!" – was the committed reaction from the larger than life senior Fianna Fáil politician.

The graceful-looking, white-painted, half-decked, diesel-engined thirty-two-footer was handed over to Martin Ferris in the month of September and was fishing oysters out of Fenit for the beginning of the season in October. Ferris was also working on the oil rigs in the Porcupine Basin off the west coast at the time. He was to take delivery of his boat at a Galway boat-building yard but could not do so because it clashed with a two-week stint on the oil exploration rig. On the day before going on the rig, he drove his brother Brian, Seanie Griffin and the late John Paul O'Mahony to Galway so that they could crew the boat down to Fenit. He dropped the three Fenit men off at the docks in Galway and he himself left for the oil rig. On returning a fortnight later, he discovered the crew still on the booze in the Aran Islands and his boat still in Galway. Naturally, he strained to hold his leadership qualities and patience intact.

But Ferris was now the contented and proud owner of his own boat, and he was looking forward to the start of the oyster season. He was elected chairman of the newly constituted Tralee Bay Oyster Protection and Conservation Association, and that was to bring its bundle of troubles as the years went on. He had borrowed the deposit for the boat from his mother and knew he was well capable of repaying the Bord Iascaigh Mhara Boat Scheme if the oyster bed problems could be resolved. He named the boat *Eamon Marie* after his wife and son.

The young boy adored his father. His love has been reciprocated throughout their lives. Eamon's success on the Gaelic football fields has given Martin immense pride. He would eventually be released for brief outings to see Eamon wearing the Kerry football jersey in Croke Park. Anyway, back in 1978, a more normal life seemed to be on the horizon for Martin. He was settling down happily with his wife, child and his new boat.

The aim of the Tralee Bay Oyster Protection and Conservation Association was to organise the number of oysters taken, the size of oyster and the number of days and hours fished on the bed.

However, because of some resistance to the rules of the association and the number of outside boats on the bay, the next three months of 1978 were testing ones on Tralee Bay for Martin Ferris. Many breaches of the fishing regulations were blamed on the so-called "outsiders". A deputation of Fenit fishermen led by Ferris had a meeting with the Board of Fisheries Conservators and bailiffs to discuss the illegal taking of small oysters from the bed by non-local boats. Sean Griffin and Ferris had, along with Fishermen's Association members, discovered several thousand undersized oysters on board the *Ocean Billiard* in November 1978. This was one of the boats named to fishery inspectors. The evidence was clear and action had to be taken.

The atmosphere was antagonistic and confrontational as clear evidence of contravention of the accepted rules was discovered on a number of outside boats. Ferris and the Fenit fishermen were concerned at seeing their industry being possibly irreparably damaged.

With tempers running high and all parties inevitably heading towards confrontation, the most serious incident of the Oyster Fishing War occurred on a frosty, calm 18 December 1978 near Fenit pier. The sizeable *Ocean Billiard* seemingly took the decision to go fishing contrary to the wishes of the association. She was steaming away from the pier area when she was in collision with the *Eamon Marie*, owned and skippered by Martin Ferris. To the shock and consternation of many other crews looking on, in just a matter of seconds the crew of the large trawler saw the water rising around their bodies as the boat sank. It was indeed serious and extremely dangerous.

Evidence given to a court afterwards disclosed that an ad hoc meeting of Fenit fishermen had been held on the sea with the boats pulling alongside each other to discuss the ongoing problem. The Fenit boats had decided to surround the *Ocean Billiard* to prevent it from fishing.

The collision resulted in the crew of the Dingle boat ending up in the icy cold December water after their boat sank. Ferris and a number of local oyster fishermen were charged with causing the collision by allegedly ramming the Dingle boat. So too were the crews of another two local boats. They were taken to Limerick Prison on remand. It was deemed too close to Christmas for a bail hearing. But considerable political string-pulling with Fianna Fáil ministers brought about a special sitting of the court on the Friday on which the courts rose for the Christmas holidays. A convoy of up to thirty cars from the parish conveyed the good news to Limerick Prison, where the bailsmen had to sign papers for the release of the Fenit fishermen. Cruises Hotel bar did a serious few hours business in celebration of having the lads out for Christmas.

Quite extraordinarily, the case was not heard for a further two years until mid-December 1980, again carrying the added fear that all of these families would have their men in jail for Christmas. The eight men charged were Martin Ferris, Mick Kelly, John Hanafin, James Ferris, Sean Griffin, James O'Shea, Joseph Walsh and Sean Murphy.

On the fifth day of the hearing, a highly respected elderly local fisherman named Dan Crowley, who was the pillar of the Labour party in Fenit, gave evidence that possibly swung the case in favour of the Fenit fishermen. It was Martin Ferris's boat the *Eamon Marie* that collided with the Dingle trawler. Dan's evidence concurred with the evidence of other accused fishermen, Joe Walsh, James O'Shea, Sean Murphy and Ferris. Crowley saw the "Dingle trawler zigzagging between the two lines of boats" which were preventing it from fishing. Other evidence stated that "O'Connor's boat was steering an irregular course and it veered towards a white boat [*Eamon Marie*] and its bow appeared to make contact."

James O'Shea said when Andrew O'Connor was in the water after his trawler sank that he offered to take Mr O'Connor on board his boat the *Ocean Mist*, but Mr

O'Connor refused the offer. Prosecuting Counsel Martin Kennedy, SC, stressed that on the day of the sinking, 18 December, Mr O'Connor had not been convicted of taking small oysters. The verdict, which was handed down on Christmas week, was "acquitted, not guilty" on all the Fenit fishermen.

The oyster problems were eventually sorted out, and today the oyster bed is harvested each year from October to around March on a quota basis. This system seems to suit everybody, and the "small oyster" is respected by all of the member fishermen.

The tragic hunger strike in which Bobby Sands was the first to die in May 1981 generated a huge outburst of emotion throughout the island of Ireland. Nine more prisoners were to die in the following months as British Prime Minister Thatcher refused to cooperate with the demands of the hunger strikers. Ferris was deeply immersed in the widespread demonstrations which the whole dreadful scenario of the deaths generated.

During the H-Block protests in 1980, the house of a retired English judge in Caragh Lake, County Kerry, was burned by the IRA. Once again Ferris was taken into custody and interrogated in Killarney Garda Barracks by gardaí who were not local. Michael Day of Ballinaskelligs was also interrogated on the same occasion, after which he was hospitalised.

In a book called *The Informer*, the author, Sean O'Callaghan from Tralee, asserted that he and Ferris were together on operations in the Carlow-Kilkenny area in 1982. It stated they had a close call in avoiding detection and capture as he, Pat Currie and Ferris traversed a river by the power of an unreliable outboard motor. Ferris and the informer were arrested in Kilkenny shortly afterwards and placed in two separate cells in the garda station. Garda sources said they had sufficient information to bring serious charges against both Ferris and O'Callaghan. However, in retrospect, Ferris can now piece together the reasons why they were not charged. He heard O'Callaghan ask for a phone, which he explained afterwards was to contact his solicitor. The phone call was taken out of Martin's hearing, and today Ferris believes the call was made to O'Callaghan's garda handler instead. The charges were pulled and the two Kerrymen were released. O'Callaghan was worth more as an informer than he would be if locked up in Portlaoise for a few years.[1]

In the same period, the Salmon Fishing War of the 1980s saw tough confrontations between the Irish navy and the coastal fishermen. There were insufficient net licences in circulation in the area, and so the local coastal men took the law into their own hands. There was almost daily interaction between the fishermen and the navy at the time, with the threat of being boarded by the navy a constant possibility at sea.

In Fenit one particular evening, a message came through on radio. It said that the navy had boarded a boat back in Brandon Bay and that there was a skirmish and that one fisherman was injured. The navy took all his fishing gear and fish and were coming in to land it all at Fenit pier.

"So, we allowed them come in so far but wouldn't let them land. There were about 80 or 90 of us on the pier at that stage."

On that evening there was horse racing at Ballybeggan Race Course in Tralee, and a message was called over the public address system asking all off-duty gardaí to report for urgent duty to Tralee Garda Station and then proceed to Fenit pier.

> Meanwhile the navy kept trying to land, but we wouldn't let them. They anchored out the bay and came in to the pier in rubber dinghies. They tried three or four times, but they couldn't land. There was a shower of stones raining down on the water every time they approached. They just couldn't get up the steps of the pier. Then we got a phone message from someone of our own lads who was at the

horse racing in Tralee confirming that garda reinforcements were on the way out to Fenit.

So we blocked the pier. Some gardaí were already out in Fenit, and so eventually there were about twenty-five to thirty gardaí and maybe up to 150 fishermen. The army were coming also, and none of them could get down the pier. We had the gates chained and barricades erected all along the pier. There were about fifteen gardaí trapped out at the head of the pier and it was getting dark.

Some of the fishermen knocked out the bulbs in the lights, and so some of the gardaí were getting uneasy about the situation. Especially when they saw some of the fishermen in balaclavas, the night getting darker and no way of getting home.

Ferris recalls the gardaí pleading, "Please lads, we want to get out of here. Tell us how we can get out of this!"

"We eventually frisked every one of them and allowed them walk through unharmed. We first got guarantees that there would be no arrests of any fishermen. Then we allowed the gardaí home. The navy had to go away too, by sea; they couldn't land. But it was a constant battle for the fishermen in those times."

On another occasion, the *Eamon Marie* was fishing salmon just north of Loop Head when Martin saw a navy corvette approaching. Her boarding boat was already launched and was heading straight for Ferris and his crew of Batt O'Shea and Kevin O'Mahony.

The Fenit crew immediately hauled their nets and opened up their throttle full steam ahead towards the coast. The navy boarding boat was closing in on them. It made numerous efforts to come alongside the Fenit boat, but Martin's crew threw out a combination rope (a nylon rope with a strand of wire going through it) and pulled it along behind them, preventing the navy sailors from getting any closer. The chase took the two boats from Loop Head across the mouth of the Shannon and around Kerry

Head. Martin then headed in through Tralee Bay on the landward side of Muchloch Rock and Oileán Bearnach. Banna Beach and Barrow Beach were looming closer, but so too were the navy. Another navy rubber dinghy was now in the chase. There is a dangerous hidden reef between Muchloch Rock and Ballyheigue Strand. Martin kept as close to the coast as was safe, but the two navy dinghies were still in hot pursuit. Ferris maintained his boat close to these rocks and then to the familiar coastline where he knew every hazard and tidal movement, thanks to his youth spent fishing with Jim Kane Ferris, but still the navy stayed in constant touch all the way.

Told in his own words, those wild days seem almost comical now, but in reality they were tough and dangerous times. There was little other work for these young men, and governments ignored their pleas for rights to fish. The corollary of that is that the young men of Fenit, too, showed scant regard for those who tried to stop them. Martin described the incident:

> They chased me from Clare the whole way into the harbour's mouth in Barrow, after they failed to board us for fishing salmon up near Loop Head. Batt O'Shea and Kevin O'Mahony were on the boat with me. The Battle of Dunleeky it was called! If you go up to Clare they still talk about it! The navy couldn't board us because we were inside against the rocks, and we came all the way down the Clare coast and we cut across the Shannon. When they tried to cut us off at the mouth of the Shannon, we threw out what is called a combination rope and towed it across in front of the navy ship. They were afraid they would pick it up in the propeller. So we got to Kerry Head and we made our way down and in along by the coast. And right over into Barrow, and they couldn't board us.
>
> We felt we were being deprived of a living by not having licences and so we fought them. They tried to

board us, and I taped a home-made gaffe on to the handle of a brush and tried to puncture the rubber dinghy. There were two rubber dinghies – one on either side. Batteen had a slash hook, and there was a blade on both sides of it, and he swiped it across the water! There was no way the navy was going to board us. It was a matter of principle. They followed us from about an hour north of Loop Head, the whole way into Oileán Bearnach. And still couldn't get aboard us. We kept them to the coast and along by the rocks. I don't think they knew the coast as well as we did. It's one of the lighter moments of my life anyway! We were in the *Eamon Marie*, my own boat. We got safely into harbour's mouth in Barrow Harbour. It was too dangerous for the navy to pursue us the whole way.

The chase was overheard on radio in Fenit port. Another Fenit boat went out to assist Martin's boat by offloading nets and catch close to the coast. However, the episode wasn't over yet. He looked up to see a number of gardaí from Tralee on top of Knockaune height, where the golf club is now. They were in readiness to take over the chase on behalf of the powers of law and order. He also saw the emerging presence of about thirty or forty Fenit fishermen rising out of the Barrow sandhills and shouting their support for their comrades.

The whole affair had been heard on VHF by the Fenit boats, and so Paudeen Kelly and the Fenit lads came around in cars. They just came out of the sandhills and came right down to the sandbanks. And they called to us, were we all right? There was always great comradeship between the fishermen in Fenit. We had a war every day with the navy because we were poaching salmon. At that time there was tremendous solidarity, because if one of us was in trouble, everybody joined in.

They brought us to court anyway, up to Kilkee.

Chapter Six

Arthur "Spanky" O'Leary from Tralee was our solicitor. So Spanky went off up in the big white Datsun. Batteen, Kevin and myself drove up, and we met him there at a hotel.

Before we went to court we went into the hotel, and Spanky had brandy and milk, and the two boys and myself had a Jameson. We went across anyway to the courthouse, and there was in fact no courthouse . . . There's no courthouse in Kilkee. There was just a grocer's shop and an old-fashioned pub in the same building. At the back of the pub, sitting in a sort of alcove, there's your man the judge, sitting down at a wooden table. The District Court was held at the back of a pub.

When we were walking up the steps to it, Spanky said to us, "Come on, come on, come on, you're all right, you'll be fine," and people were saying, "There they are, there they are." You could hear all this mumbling going on amongst the people lined up around the shop and pub for their own court cases. The case was called and it was immediately transferred to Ennis Circuit Court. The judge wouldn't try such a serious case at the back of a pub, I suppose. So, he transferred it from the Kilkee District to Ennis Circuit Court. So, he asked us what we wanted to be tried by and Spanky said, "Judge and jury."

I said to Spanky, "Are you fecking mad, a Clare jury?" I said. "They'll convict us!"

"No, no, no, you'll be dead sound. A jury won't convict you at all."

So, that was fine. We left it and came back to the hotel, and I know anyway the boys started drinking, and they drank and Spanky drank. We ran out of milk. I had to go out for more milk for Spanky's brandy. He had gone through a couple of pints of milk during the day drinking brandy. I was driving, so I just had a few bottles of Heineken or Harp. I said somebody had better stay sober. Anyway, Spanky said he was going home, and I said I would go for a drive back the coast to see the boats out fishing off the cliffs. And I did that.

So I came back and I said to myself, this is going to be an awful day. We are at it since eight o'clock in the morning, and this was three or four o'clock in the evening. Spanky was gone to catch the ferry. I think the last ferry was at half seven or eight o'clock. Off he went and we were told anyway that we had a very short time to make the ferry. We ended up in Ballybunion that night.

Due to the fallout as a consequence of the action in the following chapter and the *Marita Ann* affair, this case was never called to trial. The powers-that-be would have Ferris safely behind bars anyway, and for security reasons they would not risk bringing him to trial again for the salmon conflict.

es Mullins and Patie Ferris on their wedding day.

es and Patie Ferris with 5-month-old Martin.

Martin aged 2.

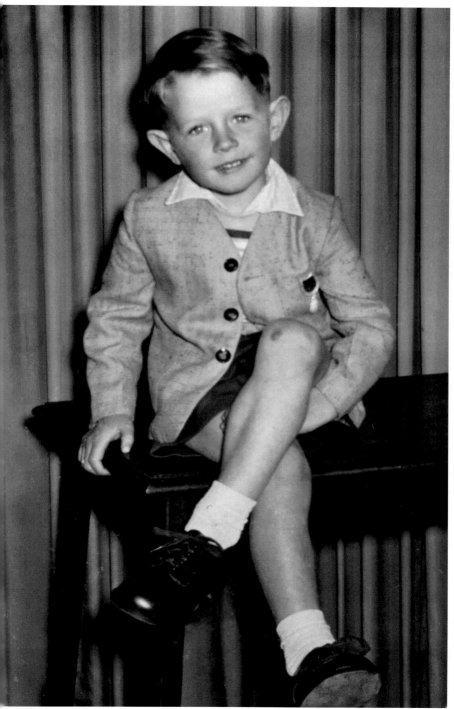

tin aged 4 and a half, 1956.

First Holy Communion, May 1959.

rtin, Aunt Molly and Brian.

Carrying the banner in a protest in support of Liam Cotter, June 1972.

Churchill Commemoration, August 1972. Mick Lynch and Batt Dowling hold wreath
speakers Charlie McGlade and George Rice are in centre, while Martin stands at top, just t
the right of the cross pillar. Paddy Kelly (in hat) stands top left; Liam Cotter directly behin
Batt Dowling.

ry Under-21 All-Ireland Winners, 1973; Martin second from the left in back row, flanked Mikey Sheehy and Tim Kennelly; Batt O'Shea kneels directly in front of Martin.

tin and Marie in 1977 a few months after his release from Portlaoise Prison.

22 May, 1978

Mr. J. J. Barrett,
Ballinasare,
Tralee,
Co. Kerry.

Dear Jo Jo.,

I have your further letter on behalf of Mr. Martin Ferris, Church Hill, Fenit, who is anxious to obtai a BIM grant and loan for the purchase of a new boat

I have asked that enquiries into this matter be expedited and I will write you again as soon as possible.

Yours sincerely,

Brian Lenihan

Minister for Fisheries

Letter from Brian Lenihan.

rice Prendergast, Martin Ferris, John Kelly and Eddie Jennings walked from Tralee to
lin dressed in blankets to highlight the 1981 hunger strike.

easa, Eamon, Oonagh and Deirdre with baby Cianán in 1983.

Guns and ammunition landed from the *Marita Ann* at Haulbowline naval base (*Cork Examiner*).

Ferris in the back of a special branch car after arrest (*Cork Examiner*).

...ving Bridewell in Cork for court hearing in Dublin (*Cork Examiner*).

...ving the Special Criminal Court after sentence, 19 December 1984.

The Ferris children on Easter Sunday, 1985: Eamon, 11, holding Cianán, 21 month; Toireasa, 5; Deirdre, 4; Oonagh, 6 and a half.

Gerry Adams and Eamon Ferris, Bodenstown, June 1986.

en visit, Portlaoise Prison, 1987: Agnes, Toireasa, Martin and Cianán.

n visit, Portlaoise Prison: Martin and Marie with Deirdre, Toireasa and Oonagh in 1989.

Open visit, Portlaoise Prison: Martin and Toireasa in May 1989.

Martin and Máirtín together for the first time outside prison, on the occasion of the fune of his mother, Agnes.

daughter Oonagh at the graveside at his mother's funeral, 28 January 1989.

Martin and Brian shouldering the coffin at the funeral of their mother Agnes.

Brian, Martin and son Eamon after Martin got parole to watch Eamon play for Kerry i
the Vocational Schools All-Ireland Final at Croke Park in 1990.

blican prisoners in Portlaoise in 1990; Martin fourth from the left in the front row.

publican prisoners in Portlaoise in 1991; Martin second from the right in the front row.

Martin on parole for Cianán's First Holy Communion in 1991: Martin amd Marie w
Toireasa, Cianán, Oonagh, Deirdre, Eamon and Máirtín.

Republican prisoners' GAA team which played a Pat Critchley Laois selection in
Portlaoise Prison in 1992. Front: Paudge Lavin, Brian McQuaid, Don McEvoy,
Nicky Kehoe, "Benzini" Murphy; back: Martin Ferris, Arnie O'Connell, Anto
Beggs, Eamonn Nolan, Seamus Clarke.

ber 1994 Earl of Desmond Hotel welcome-back do for Martin Ferris attended by Johnny
er of the Birmingham Six; also in picture is Kerry republican Gerry Savage (*Kerry's Eye*).

Stormont in September 1997, with Caoimhín Ó Caoláin, Gerry Adams, Lucilita
athnach and Martin McGuinness.

With Martin McGuinness, Joe Cahill, Gerry Adams and Pat Doherty.

al opening of Sinn Féin office, Tralee, 1999: Martin Ferris, Gerry Savage, Gerry Adams, cillor Tony Curtin and Councillor Cathal Foley.

election count in Tralee, 1999.

At the Kerry North election count: Thomas McEllistrim, Martin Ferris, Martin McGuinn

Democratic Party presidential candidate John Kerry in the USA, March 2003.

anddaughter Caoilfhinn's baptism, October 2004. Back: Máirtín, Cianán, Martin hold-
aby Earnan, Eamon; front Rita (Marie's mother), Marie holding Caoilfhinn, Deirdre,
gh, Toireasa.

Celebrating the appointment of Toireasa as Mayor of Kerry. Back: Eamon, Oonagh, Mar
Deirdre and Cianán Ferris; front: Margaret "Gargy" Hoare, Toireasa and Marie Fer
(*Kerry's Eye*).

CHAPTER SEVEN

IN SEPTEMBER 1984, Martin Ferris engaged in possibly the most dangerous and daring escapade undertaken by him as an IRA volunteer. He attempted to import seven tons of arms and ammunition by dangerously trans-shipping the cargo under atrocious conditions in the Atlantic Ocean. It was a cargo of arms which the IRA need-ed, and the whole operation had the sanction and blessing of the highest level in the IRA. To successfully undertake the operation, Ferris would need an ocean-going trawler, and so he joined up with fellow Fenit IRA Volunteer Mike Browne, who was skipper of a trawler named *Marita Ann*. Although the trawler was forty-five years old and had never been out so far in the Atlantic, Martin was confident that Mike was a highly competent and much trusted fishing skipper and would be well capable of dealing with any imponderables in the dangerous operation.

The plan was for the *Marita Ann* to rendezvous in the Atlantic with the arms-carrying, Boston-registered trawler named the *Valhalla*. The task was an enormous one, because the *Marita Ann* was an old boat and the weather conditions would have to be suitable for any trans-shipping of cargo in the high seas. When transferred to the *Marita Ann*, the shipment was to be landed on the south Kerry coastline where a number of vehicles were on stand-by to take the arms to various safe arms dumps. The skipper of the *Valhalla* was the experienced Captain Bob Anderson, a stereotypical sea captain with a vast knowledge of the seas off the north-eastern American coast.

"A powerfully built six-footer, of Norwegian ancestry, [he] was an orphan of this proud tradition. His heritage ran in a direct line from the buccaneers of old to the rum-runners of a less-distant past. Anderson was a modern-day maritime soldier of fortune, ferrying whatever would bring the best price."[1]

They had the outline of the overall plan worked out, but it would necessitate much detailed organising before the two boats would be ready to sail from their two respective ports on either side of the Atlantic. From his viewpoint, Ferris was secure in the knowledge that he had a boat worthy of doing this specific trip, and he had the right man in Mike Browne at the helm. Most importantly, Mike Browne was a committed republican, an expert on diesel engines and a first class navigator. Nothing would deter Martin and Mike at that stage.

During the build-up to the shipment, Martin Ferris was under instructions to prepare with Mike Browne and the transport on land for the major mission. He had secured the reasonably seaworthy trawler, of course, as the first requirement, and he was confident that the experienced fisherman, Michael Browne, from a well respected Fenit fishing family, could deliver whatever was asked of him. Some thought the *Marita Ann* was too old for such a hazardous voyage, but Ferris and Browne had exceptional courage, a thorough knowledge of the sea, and Browne was a highly capable navigator and seagoing skipper. They both had a deep love of the sea.

Chapter Seven

On St Patrick's Day 1984, a meeting was held in Galway where all of the initial planning took place. Present at the meeting were all personnel essential to the upcoming operation, including the two skippers – Mike Browne and Captain Bob Anderson. For navigational purposes it was essential that Anderson and Browne would have a lengthy discussion to arrange the point of contact in the Atlantic. But most importantly, they needed to devise a means by which they could transfer the seven ton cargo of arms from ship to ship on the high seas. Anderson wanted Browne's *Marita Ann* to come out six hundred miles from Ireland. Browne doubted if his sixty-five-foot-long trawler was capable of making such a long voyage into the Atlantic in September weather. After much "iffing and anding", and considerable "effing and blinding", Browne stuck to his guns and convinced Anderson to come to an agreed point approximately two hundred miles from Ireland. Nobody underestimated the difficulty involved, but in all calculations the weather forecast would play a vital role. Survival in the Atlantic in a sixty-five-foot timber-hulled trawler requires no small amount of luck. The clemency of the elements is a basic requirement. The ferocity of the storms could be fatal. So, the timing of the voyages was going to be crucial. You don't go out there in December.

Enjoying himself there amongst the St Patrick's Day celebrations, with his shamrock-emblazoned sweater and hat, Bob Anderson faded into the crowd of American tourists enjoying the parade and festivities. His seemingly innocent presence in Galway did not reveal to the Special Branch that the real reason for his visit there was to meet with some of the top IRA men in the country.

The arrangements were tentatively made, but unavoidable delays of all descriptions, on both sides of the Atlantic, continuously postponed the operation from month to month. It was looking dangerously like the hurricane season off the coast of the United States might cause a major change of plans until safer, more predictable weather in

1985. Eventually, it was agreed that sometime late in September, although extremely risky, could still allow a window of opportunity in which to proceed with the daring plan. But the same window of opportunity in September might also deliver a seven-day hurricane blowing off the east coast of the USA. It is a very uncertain time of year off the east coast of America in the Atlantic. Contact indicated it was getting extremely close to the starter's flag being raised. Again, in horse-racing parlance, once the Boston ship went to sea, Martin Ferris was then under starter's orders, and no matter what the weather he would have to embark on his side of the mission from Ireland.

On 11 and 12 September 1984, the *Valhalla* picked up twenty-six tons of crushed ice at Gloucester port as any fishing trawler would do when preparing for a prolonged fishing voyage. She also took on board 7,899 gallons of fuel at Gloucester Marine Railways in preparation for some offshore sword fishing. At least that was the cover story Anderson was using along the Gloucester waterfront. The *Valhalla* headed out of Gloucester port on 14 September at one o'clock in the morning. Anderson had the most part of 2,000 dangerously tough miles ahead. The *Valhalla* was to encounter some terrible weather and suffered heavy damage to the wheelhouse. A member of the *Valhalla* crew, John McIntyre from Boston, told Martin that they were lucky to escape serious tragedy. The craft nearly got swamped by a freak wave in that outward trip. The windows in the wheelhouse were driven in by the giant wave and all the electrics went out. They said it was a massive wave. They were very lucky. Used to heavy seas while fishing two to three hundred miles off Newfoundland, Anderson had been brave enough to continue and keep his rendezvous point with Martin Ferris, Mike Browne and company.

In Kerry, without drawing any unnecessary attention around Fenit port, Ferris discreetly prepared for the voyage. Naturally, a part of the preparation was a simple checklist of items for a week at sea. Those goods had to be bought from a republican sympathiser who would not ask awkward questions. They knew the voyage would take them away for a number of days and that they had to travel beyond 150 miles west of Ireland to collect the arms. The long-range weather forecasts were bad. They got ready for the operation. The *Valhalla* was well out in the Atlantic by now but was maintaining radio silence for security purposes. Due to the amount of coordination necessary, much still hung in the balance until Ferris travelled to Dublin and met his IRA contact on Saturday night.

Under cover of the All-Ireland Final between Kerry and Dublin to be played in Croke Park on 23 September, Ferris made his final arrangements with Northern Command. The great Kerry team of the 1970s was striving to regain its power again after losing in 1982 and 1983. They were back in the "Centenary" final again in '84 against the All-Ireland champions, Dublin.

Ferris had travelled to Dublin just as any keen follower of Kerry football. Had his IRA activities not absorbed his life, he might well have been playing for Kerry. On Saturday night he met with his contact person in a hotel in the north side of the city. The update was confirming exactly Mike Browne's predetermined rendezvous arrangements with Captain Anderson. He confirmed to Ferris that the *Valhalla* was on its way. They expected it at the rendezvous point in the Atlantic on about the following Wednesday or Thursday. Mike was aware of the whole plan from a navigational point of view. In fact, only he and Anderson were fully aware of the exact location where the ships would meet. They were also the sole possessors of the radio code words to be used when the vessels got safely close to within a certain radio band. Martin and his contact agreed everything and shook hands.

The match was on the following day, and Kerry and Dublin jerseys were everywhere. There was a great atmosphere in Dublin city. Martin found that he could not enjoy it, he had so much on his mind. Phones were not safe, so

Mike was at home in Fenit anxiously waiting for Martin to physically return with the information as to whether the action was going ahead or not.

During that period, Mike normally fished his trawler out of Fenit. Johnny McCarthy and Gavin Mortimer, two young Fenit lads, were his regular crew members. About a week earlier Mike had asked Martin if it was okay to tell the crew to turn up for the voyage. The IRA had offered them a group of ten able and experienced men from outside of Kerry for crewing and for moving the arms to dumps. Martin declined; they would have been too easily identifiable in Kerry due to the constant garda surveillance. Martin told Mike, "Whatever we do, we'll leave things as normal as possible." He had said not to do anything different and that he himself would deal with the crew when he met them.

Martin went to the match, and saw Kerry beat Dublin in a display of forward power in which Eoin Liston scored three goals and four points. Mikey Sheehy carved his name into football legend once more with the possible goal of the century from a free-kick. His Austin Stacks clubmate Ger Power had created the free-kick and also had a stormer of a performance. The celebrations would go on long into the night and early morning, but Martin left it all behind him and returned home directly afterwards, getting a drive to Kerry that night. He rose early the next morning and went to see Mike Browne. Following on his meeting in Dublin, he explained that it was full steam ahead and what was now to be done. Mike said that one of his crew, Gavin Mortimer, was in Dublin at the match and that he would not be back until that night. Mike and Martin agreed to leave on the Monday night. As a result of Martin's information, Mike went ahead finalising the boat. Martin collected a rifle and ammunition from a safe spot in Churchill near his homeplace. Mike went away and got money and food.

The twenty-one foot punt was borrowed from Martin's pal Batt O'Shea and was secured to the deck after Johnny

Mac had brought it down to the boat. Batt O'Shea was unaware of the use it would be put to in the Atlantic. He thought it was going to Carrigaholt for use in a painting job to be done to the *Marita Ann*. Batt O'Shea, from the Spa, and Martin were very close friends. They had played Gaelic football together down the years and in fact won an All-Ireland Under-21 medal together with a star-studded Kerry team in 1973.

When leaving Marie at home, Martin told her he was going on a fishing trip. She recalls:

> I can remember it was Monday that Martin left on the "fishing trip". Of course what I know now is that it wasn't a fishing trip at all. I did not know he was on a big operation. My first sign of pregnancy always was a heartburn. It was the only time I ever got it. On the Sunday evening I can remember saying, "Oh, my God, I've got heartburn."
>
> "Do you think you're pregnant?" Martin said.
>
> "I probably am."
>
> And it was the following day that he left. He told me, "Look, I am going away. I'll see you Friday."
>
> "Fine," I said, but then he gave me a time, which was most unusual. Martin would never give me a time.
>
> "Look, I'll be home around 11 o'clock on Friday night."
>
> Now, I'm not foolish, I knew something important was cooking, but I hadn't a clue what it was. I said, "Fine."

Preparations for food on board had to be good. They didn't know how long they were going to be out there. They thought it might be three days, but they got enough grub for a week. Mike had filled the boat with diesel. Everything was ready. They needed nearly a thousand pounds cash between diesel and everything else for the operation in the week ahead.

That was all right, but there was no sign of Gavin. So Ferris was impatiently waiting until eventually at ten o'clock or so Gavin and Brian landed in Churchill.

> I just said to Gavin, "Mike was looking for you. He said he wants to see you; he said it's urgent."
>
> Gavin said, "Right!"
>
> So I asked Brian to take the car and drop Gavin back to the pier.
>
> I stayed around for a while. Johnny McCarthy carried the punt away from my mother's house and brought it down aboard the *Marita Ann*, moored at about midway on the Main Pier. The weather forecast was not looking too kind, and in normal circumstances the *Marita Ann* would not have put to sea.

However, with the *Valhalla* now at sea for almost ten days in bad weather, it was vital that *Marita Ann* would get under way very soon. Martin felt he had everything he needed on board.

He believes it was 12.45 a.m., and there wasn't a sinner around the docks. There was an angler fishing away out at the head of the pier, which wouldn't be unusual, and the two crew members, Gavin Mortimer and Johnny McCarthy, were on board. Mike Browne was also on board. It was very quiet and peaceful with a slight breeze blowing across the shelter of the harbour. Mike had seen Martin driving up the pier. Although it was a beautiful, calm night in Fenit, that can change in a matter of minutes. Mike expressed his concern about the weather. He had been listening to the Trawler Band radio weather forecast system. The forecast was ominously poor for September. However, Ferris and Browne could not leave the *Valhalla* waiting around in the Porcupine Basin in such bad weather. It was a predicament, but Martin and Mike decided to put to sea. The leader of the operation recalls:

> Mike went into the wheelhouse. He knew well what to do. So I just ripped off the ropes from the bollards

on the pier, fore and aft, and I jumped down into the *Marita Ann*. The two boys, Johnny and Gavin, were gone away to bunk. I never said anything to them at this stage, although it would be very unusual for me to be crewing with them on Mike's boat. We drew away from the pier wall and rounded the green light at the head of the pier. That solitary figure was angling near the head of the pier under the green light.

Martin often pondered afterwards on this lone figure with a fishing rod. Was he significant in their later capture? They steamed full-ahead due south-west of the Samphire Rock. Before long they had put the Fenit Lighthouse on Little Samphire behind them, and they were heading west along Tralee Bay. Lights of houses were dotted all along the coastline from Derrymore to Castlegregory and sweeping back to mighty Brandon Head beyond. The lights of the odd car could be seen on the Tralee to Dingle road rising up towards Camp, Gleann na nGealt and on towards Annascaul.

They were now well back the bay heading north-west. It was in the same area of Tralee Bay in which Roger Casement had transferred from the U-boat to the landing punt on his return to Ireland for the 1916 Rising. It was here also that the steamer, the *Aud*, came nosing her way through the waters off Fenit, unaware that the expected welcoming signal lights would never shine for her. All those years ago, the ship had appeared in Tralee Bay in preparation to land her cargo of arms for the Easter Rising of 1916. Her efforts were to be aborted off County Cork a few days later when, under arrest by the British navy, she was scuttled by her skipper, Karl Spindler.

It would soon be time for Martin to apprise the two unknowing crew members, Johnny and Gavin, of the situation in which they were to play a part.

Martin said to Mike:

"I am going to call the two boys up and put them in the picture." So, I called the two lads up and I told them, "I am sorry about this, lads; I am on an IRA operation and Mike Browne is on an IRA operation. We will be back some time later on this week." I said, "You know, lads, basically, we are leaving it up to yourselves. But, I am hoping that you will help me. There will be a lot of heavy work, and it could be tricky." They agreed to help me out, and they did, and they were brilliant.

Johnny McCarthy would say years later, in 2003, that he believed Martin Ferris was the finest man he ever met and that he would do anything for him if asked, then or now.

So, the *Marita Ann* headed out into the Atlantic, leaving the powerful shoulders of Brandon Head and Kerry Head, on each side of Tralee Bay and Brandon Bay, well behind them. Their voyage of an estimated twenty-four hours steaming was well under way, into the unknown, a distance into the Atlantic which none of them had ever travelled by sea before.

They had crossed the mouth of the Shannon and put Loop Head Lighthouse behind them too. At approximately twenty-three miles north of the Blasket Islands and ten miles off the Clare coast, they picked up their course for rendezvous, now approximately a full day's treacherous steaming away. *Marita Ann* had made good progress for the first six hours, but a slight engine problem needed attention. This meant cutting her engines and heaving-to, side-on to the heavy seas. This is a dangerous manoeuvre in any size of boat. The weather was getting heavier, and they needed half a day to get the engine up to required performance again. Their rendezvous point was 178 miles west of the Blaskets at a point 52°30' north and 14°10' west. They had allowed themselves enough time to reach the rendezvous area, so getting the engine running right was comfortable but for the risk of being side-on to these increasingly heavy waves. The strong gale eventually abated sufficiently to allow them to continue.

The *Marita Ann* ploughed onwards through heavy seas

towards their destination. They reached target point by Wednesday morning early. They then had to steam circuitously in the area of the appointed location until Thursday. A storm rose again and they had to heave-to in some atrocious weather until the other ship made contact with them. The first contact came around 4 p.m. on Thursday on the radio, and it was coded in a prearranged code. Mike Browne was handling the communications. From their respective nautical positions, he estimated that they were about six hours away. Their goal was about to be realised. Much rested on their shoulders, and although the adrenalin was flowing, they were aware of the huge responsibility. If they could successfully land this consignment of arms, it would be immensely important to the war effort.

Mike estimated the expected time of rendezvous and Martin concurred. He went out on deck and was sitting on a bale of rope, just thinking, while the two boys, Gavin and Johnny, went away to bunk. It was nasty weather, very nasty. It was dry, but an uncomfortable force six wind and high seas kept Martin tense. As usual, Mike was ably in control of the boat in the wheelhouse.

So Ferris was sitting there and he heard the drone of an engine. Out of nowhere a plane came upon them and flew directly over the *Marita Ann*. Martin explains:

> It was possibly just a couple of hundred feet in the air above us. "God!" I said, "That's a strange one anyway." She seemed to come from nowhere. I had worked on the oil rigs out there in the Porcupine and I often saw NATO exercises and so forth. I often witnessed NATO manoeuvres with planes involved. Then there were planes which regularly came out to monitor the weather for forecasting purposes. So, I thought to myself, maybe it was one of those. Of course, I know now that this was probably the first strike by the British.
>
> The plane was a Nimrod, but I didn't know that when I saw it first. I only found that out later. So,

anyway, I sat there pondering on the weather and wondering if it would be possible to transfer the arms under such ugly weather conditions. It was about 10 or 11 p.m. when we saw the other boat coming and we made radio contact again.

The presence of the plane bothered Martin. John Crawley was the one who identified the Nimrod. He said he knew those aircraft well. It had flown away for about an hour and come back again, and then it disappeared. Ferris feared something was wrong, and he didn't want to say or think the unthinkable, but after Anderson had brought such a substantial quantity of arms and ammunition from the States, how could he refuse to take it on board? He was very aware of how important this consignment would be to the struggle, and an instant decision had to be made. Ferris took the decision to take the gear.

Such was the severity of the sea that it was impossible for the two craft to offload the cargo by pulling alongside. They decided there was no way in the world that they could go alongside for a gunwale-to-gunwale transfer. Three or four attempts convinced them of that. It was much too rough. With the two vessels pitching and rolling ten feet up and the other ten feet down into troughs, the big lorry tyres that Mike had brought along as fenders were essentially ineffective under these conditions. On one much too close attempt, they heard a cracking of timber, and Mike Browne guessed it wasn't on the *Valhalla*, because she had a steel rim around her hull. With Mike aware that he could be holed below the sea line, they were forced to cut the nylon ropes and back away before either boat would break up. But Captain Anderson on the *Valhalla* was irate at this pull-back manoeuvre, and there were cross words exchanged between Browne and Anderson. The Fenit skipper was unwilling to risk his boat and the safety of his crew.

They had earlier ruled out the risking of lives by using the outboard motor, which Batt O'Shea had loaned

Martin, and so they just used pure old-fashioned man-power to haul the loads of arms instead. They launched the punt in the water and it was pulled across to the *Valhalla*. The gear was loaded into the punt and then it was hauled back over by the crew of the *Marita Ann*. They would then unload the guns and gear. The *Valhalla* crew would pull the empty punt over again and so on until they had all the gear transferred to the *Marita Ann*. The transfer took about seven or eight hours, and it was a tor-turous job. Meanwhile Mike Browne and Captain Anderson maintained the two boats from about fifty to one hundred feet apart, by driving the engines, nose into the weather, and keeping the heads of both vessels apart at all times. It was highly dangerous. It was a magnificent feat of seamanship and of the control of the respective vessels by both skippers.

When the transfer was complete, the *Valhalla* steamed off towards Boston and the *Marita Ann* set her nose for home and proceeded towards Ireland. At that stage there was a very rough sea running, and there were twenty to twenty-five foot waves. It was very bad, with a big swell and a lot of wind. Also, Martin recalls, there was a big ocean-going trawler working away off from them, possibly a couple of miles. They could see it was drifting closer. By the time they completed the transfer, it was within maybe a quarter of a mile of them. That again stuck in Martin's mind afterwards. What bothered him was the way they worked towards the *Marita Ann*. The shore angler on the pier at Fenit, the Nimrod and the trawler all cast some doubt in his mind for some years later. They could see that trawler was hauling its nets, but it came very close to them. The trawler eventually came so close that Martin could actually see the men on deck. For many years afterwards in Portlaoise, he wondered about that trawler and whether it was linked to the Nimrod.

That was into Friday morning, and they were heading off for the coast of Ireland, about 175 miles away. The operation had started at around 11 p.m. on Thursday night, and they had the cargo loaded by 5 a.m. on Friday morning. They were well on their way for the Irish coast at 5.30 a.m. In the heavy seas they nearly lost one of the weapons. Part of it tumbled out and it fell off the *Marita Ann*, but fortunately it landed in the punt.

The Skellig Rocks off the coast of south Kerry in the south of Ireland was the arranged point of contact with the IRA units ashore. Once they got to the Skellig, they had a further contact location further in ashore, not too far from that point. It would be less than a nautical hour from there.

Mike Browne and the lads went for a well-deserved rest to bunk. Martin Ferris was at the wheel and they were working their way home. Coming up to 5 o'clock in the evening, it was getting dark. They had another six or seven hours steaming to reach their goal before starting to unload to the motor transport which would carry the shipment to their arms dumps. A number of arms dumps had been prepared in south Kerry, and about a dozen volunteers were ready to manhandle the arms from the *Marita Ann* to the transport.

Johnny and Gavin went down to the galley at about nine o'clock to prepare a meal. At 11 p.m. Martin paid a brief visit to the galley and the boys were eating heartily. They came back up at midnight. Ferris was still at the wheel. He was heading in towards the coast, and Valentia was to the north-east of him. He was coming in south of Valentia, heading for the Skellig Rocks. Mike Browne's prearranged radio signal for the contact ashore was to be sent when the *Marita Ann* was two hours from her destination: "Hello Tom, hello Tom, hello Tom!" Browne was to say he had left on a fishing trip two hours ago. This would mean that they would be landing in two hours.

In the shadow of these rocky giants of outcrop, eight miles off the coast, lay the future of Martin Ferris's life for the next ten years. The Irish navy was on high alert and waiting to pounce. Two navy warships lay camouflaged behind the Skellig Rocks. A third vessel was close by nearer to Valentia.

The informer, Sean O'Callaghan, had been one of the last people to speak to Martin Ferris before the *Marita Ann* sailed from Fenit pier. He had done his job well and informed his garda handler. The navy vessels were well prepared and briefed. LE *Aisling*, under Lieutenant Commander J. Robinson, and LE *Emer*, under Lieutenant Commander B. Farrell, had left Haulbowline with gardaí on board both vessels. Lieutenant Commander Farrell was officer in tactical command (OTC). Both ships had patrolled together for a number of days, awaiting the arrival of the *Marita Ann*, as the esimated time of arrival (ETA) and destination were not exactly known. On the last day of the operation, the OTC was advised that the *Marita Ann*'s destination was the Kenmare River. He deployed the *Emer* on the northern side of the bay and assigned the southern side to the *Aisling*. Both ships were at action stations and prepared for boarding.

The *Marita Ann* was now nearing her destination, and Martin still was very uneasy within himself. There was just something picking at him. He had a gut feeling that things were not right. John Crawley, Johnny and Gavin came up on deck, and he asked them to get the hatch covers open and to start putting the gear on deck. He was going down to have a cup of tea and would be back up in a few minutes to help them arrange the gear. They were approximately an hour away from the Kenmare River.

Martin recalls the moment they realised they were in trouble:

> I just had the cup of tea to my lips when Gavin ran down into the galley calling me. He said, "Come up quickly. There are lights all over the place!" I said, "What!" He said to come up quickly. I ran up the deck. I was looking out at a big flashing light beaming down at us. At that stage we were about half a mile – maybe three quarters of a mile – off the

Skellig. We were about two miles inside the Irish waters limit – maybe two miles and a quarter. So obviously what happened was that the Irish navy had positioned two vessels – two navy war ships – and apparently there was a third one standing by in Valentia. Altogether, they had three of them in the area. Two of them were hidden behind Skellig Michael. Our radar would only pick up the bigger object which was the rock. They came right out from behind the cover of the rock, and they ghosted right out to us. I think that's how they did it so effectively. There were rumours afterwards about how they could blot out our radar, but that was media speculation. What I discovered afterwards was that radar would pick up the big Skelligs Rock at that distance. Only the rock and not the two Irish navy ships. The big boats would be blocked out, and that's how they came up on us. The lights were shining blindingly down on the deck, and I said, "Feck it," to myself. The second ship was now after us too.

Ferris continues:

They were probably within thirty to forty metres off us, that close, and I said to Mike, "Go west, go west! Put her full ahead!" and we started veering off out to the west, south-west. But they kept putting their nose across our bow, so we ended up going around in a half circle, trying to avoid the navy ship. We kept pushing her ahead, and they were forcing their bow across us all the time, and we just hadn't enough power or speed to get away. We wouldn't be able to compete with their engines anyway. So we kept trying and trying, but the engine was roaring and they were shouting, "Cut your engines! Cut your engines!" At that stage the other one was behind us. They were shouting through a loudhailer or megaphone. They said, "Irish Navy. We want to board you; cut your engines immediately, cut your engines. Everybody out on deck."

They were on the radio to us as well. So Mike Browne switched channels and got on to our contact ashore. He told them we were in trouble, get away to hell out of there.

"Get out to hell, we are caught, we are gone, just get away."

He got a confirmation back that the message was received and the people ashore managed to escape safely. There would have been about a dozen volunteers ashore for the operation, as back-up to help us to remove the arms and gear. If we could not alert them to our plight, then they would have been exposed also.

Anyway, for about five or so minutes we kept trying to get away, and next thing they opened up with gunfire. We were still trying to escape for open water when tracers went across our bow. Suddenly some volleys struck the wheelhouse and some rounds actually came very close, in the wheelhouse. The wheelhouse was only sheeted with tin in places, so Mike asked me if he would cut the engine. I said right, and Mike cut the engine. I said, "Mike, can you sink her?" and he said, "Yes, I can." But the pipe to scuttle her was too small. Now the only other way we could do it was with grenades, but, contrary to what was said, there were no grenades. There were grenade casings, but there were no grenades. If we had a grenade, we would throw one forward and blow the bow and she would sink maybe in a few minutes. But, we ran down anyway to see if there was any possible way to scuttle her. There was a pipe about one inch in diameter, and I said, "That's the only thing I can see." I said, "Oh, for God's sake, Mike, they'll be aboard any minute!" and I asked, "How long will it take her to go down?"

He replied, "Maybe four or five hours."

I said, "What's the depth of water here?"

He looked at the radar and the sounding and he said, "I think there's about 120 feet of water."

"Mike," I said, "the game is up!"

So, we came on deck anyway, and at that stage the navy dinghies were on both sides of us and the navy were boarding over the side. We didn't fire at the boarding party, and this was lucky because we would have been outgunned. They were aboard us anyway, and they forced us back to the stern. There was a Detective McGillicuddy and Inspector Eric Ryan. So they came over the side into the boat. Ryan was the Cork footballer in the 1950s and '60s. At first I thought they were armed soldiers, Army Rangers – the boys said they were Rangers – but they weren't. They were ordinary sailors with blackened faces in some sort of naval combat gear. I couldn't be certain what they were. I was trying to watch everything and it was happening so fast, it was just a blurred moment. I saw some of their faces were blackened. And the next thing there was another dinghy coming and two of the navy sailors were thrown out of the dinghy into the water. There was total panic amongst the boarding parties. There were two of them in the water. They were nearly gone and there was sheer panic. 'Tis like everything stood still for me. I just watched everything around me and they were shouting and running about the deck. They were threatening us with guns. It was chaotic. I was just watching everything around me – the commotion and panic was totally mad. There were two of them still in the water and they had to pull them in – they were very lucky. One of them was nearly gone. They pulled them into the dinghy, and then they had to go back to the naval ship and off-load them. Anyway, eventually they got us back astern and they tied us up with ropes. There was all this happening and the boat was rolling badly. The scuppers on both sides of the decks were taking in water, and the water was coming in one side and going out the other side and vice versa. The *Marita Ann* was broadside on the whole time. The seas now were fairly rough. It was force six or seven at around that time – as it was confirmed in court afterwards.

They were searching the *Marita Ann*, and next thing Eric Ryan and McGillicuddy opened the hatch and looked down. Then they came back and they carried out Mike Browne, and pointing through the hatch to the hold full of guns and gear, they said, "What's that?" Mike didn't answer. And then they came again and they brought all the lads up one at a time asking the same question. The boys said they didn't know. Then they brought Martin from the back of the boat from where he'd been lying on the deck aft behind the wheelhouse. The lads were in front of the wheelhouse. They brought him down into the hold. He remembers Eric Ryan saying to him:

"What is that there? What is that?" And I wouldn't look down; I was looking out, looking out towards the sea. He caught my head to force my head down and he couldn't do it. I kept my head up and tried to head-butt him, as my hands were tied behind my back, and he said, "You bastard, what is that?" he said. "Are there explosives down there?" There was sheer panic. They were afraid there were explosives down there. And I wasn't inclined to answer.

I just refused to answer. Just before they got aboard us, I had a few seconds to talk to Johnny and Gavin. They rushed over and asked what are they to say. I said, "Say nothing." I said, "Don't talk to them, say nothing." And I said, "I promise you I will do my best to get you out of this. I promise you that!" I said. "Don't say anything." And to their credit neither of them opened their mouths.

> Amongst all the confusion they left us there, hands tied behind us and lying face down on an old bale of nets and ropes at the back of the *Marita Ann*. I was talking to the lads, and the navy and gardaí were trying to tell us to shut up. We kept talking to the lads, telling them not to feckin' worry about them, and we were singing "Take it Down from the Mast, Irish Traitors", and all the boys joined in, so we sang it as best we could. What more could we do? The bit of defiance was important – to show a bit of defiance and belief that it wasn't all up for us. We were simply trying to raise our own morale.

Possibly the most dangerous aspect of their voyage was yet to occur for Martin: the transfer to the naval vessels. Martin takes it up:

> Eventually, they decided to transfer us into the navy ships. At that stage there were three navy ships around us. I was the first one they decided to move. They brought me to the side of the *Marita Ann*, and they had the dinghy down below me bobbing and rolling in the rough water. They were trying to figure out how to get me over the gunwale, with my hands tied, down the outside of the *Marita Ann* and into the dinghy. It was a tricky situation for them. Already one of the dinghies had lost two sailors, and it was almost lost itself; another nearly capsized, and here they were going to put me into another fecking dinghy with my hands still tied behind my back. *If I get into this thing I'll be lucky!* I thought to myself. So, one of the officers saw the impossibility of the task. He said to me, "I'm going to have to untie your hands." And he cocked the gun and put it up to my head. "If you as much as make a move, I'll blow your head off!"

He was the same officer as had pursued the *Eamon Marie* from above Loop Head into Barrow Harbour in the so-called "Battle of Dunleeky" in the previous June. They recognised each other immediately. Martin continues:

> They had untied the ropes and put me lying down inside in the belly of the dinghy, and he had a gun up to the back of my head. The floor of the dinghy was awash with water, and when it rolled it took in more water. The short journey to the corvette only took maybe a minute or a minute and a half to get across, but it was wet. So now I'm landed on board the corvette. Then Gavin came aboard. Gavin and myself were in one corvette and Johnny Mac and John Crawley were on board the other one. As skipper, they had to keep Mike Browne on board the *Marita Ann*, for insurance purposes or some such reason. They asked him to steer the *Marita Ann*, but he wouldn't do it. He sat down at the back of the boat and he wouldn't cooperate with them in any way. Mike knew his boat inside out, but others would find great difficulty in priming her along. And he wouldn't tell them how to do anything. They eventually had to take her in tow. But they still had trouble pumping the water out because it was an unreliable "automatic" pump, and he wouldn't tell them how to work that either.
>
> So they headed off anyway for Cork, I'd say around five o'clock in the morning. 'Twas seven o'clock that evening before we got into Cobh. 'Twas an awfully slow, fecking torturous trip. They brought us down into one of the cabins. There were double bunks, one at the top and one at the bottom. We were tied and then they tied ropes all around the bunks. It was a cage made of ropes. There was only a small porthole. We had just a washbasin, and there was no toilet in the cabin. There were two armed sailors guarding us. They were sitting in chairs, and at all times some one of them had his rifle pointing at us. This for the whole fourteen hours or whatever time

the journey took. They were ordinary naval ratings probably. I don't know what rank they would be, but they were nervous. It was probably the first time ever that they were in a situation like that. But they were sitting there with the guns pointing at us the whole way. It was a bad trip because I was fecked with asthma. It didn't help anyway with the ropes all round us and we confined to the cabin. I don't know where they thought we were going to go, even if we were to get out of the cabin.

Eventually we got to the naval base at Haulbowline–Cobh, and they took us off the naval vessels. One at a time. The navy then handed us over to the Special Branch, and we were taken by road to Cork.

The gardaí took custody of Martin, Gavin, Johnny Mac and John Crawley at Cobh, and from there they were taken to the Bridewell in Cork where they were put into the cells on Saturday night. The gardaí started questioning them, and they told Martin that his brother Brian had been arrested, that he had been picked up with another person and a man by the name of Tom Jones from Lauragh. They were stopped in a car owned by Jones somewhere down around Bantry. They were taken to Bantry Garda Barracks. Martin says that Tom Jones was one of the greatest people he ever met in his life. It was the first time Tom was ever arrested.

Jones said to the gardaí: "Under arrest for what? I don't know those two fellows at all. I just picked them up back the road when they were hitching. I just gave them a drive as I was going to Bantry."

After Tom Jones and the boys were arrested in Bantry, the gardaí went into Martin and said, "Ah, we have the whole lot of you now. We have your brother, we have another fellow, and we have an idiot who was duped into giving them a drive." That's what they were saying to Martin at that stage. Seemingly, the gardaí didn't connect Jones with them at all. Nobody pretended otherwise, and

Jones got away clean. When he died three years ago, Martin gave the oration at his funeral in Lauragh, County Kerry.

Meanwhile Marie was going through her own bad time. She was by this time frantic with worry. She was unable to sleep on the Friday night as her sixth sense told her something was not right. Added to that, she was also feeling the first signs of pregnancy. She was becoming very anxious. She was expecting him home but, unusually, she had not heard from him since Monday.

"At 11.30 on Friday night I thought, *he's not coming.* And then I went to bed, and I distinctly remember at twenty past twelve I started getting massive stomach cramps, and being alone I said, "My God, where is he? I think I'm having a miscarriage." It was exactly the same time as Martin and the *Marita Ann* were encountering the navy ship *Emer* at sea. "The pains got worse and worse and worse. So I got up and started walking around the house, and at ten to one it stopped – just stopped – the pains just stopped and at that stage – I don't know whether it is women's intuition – but I knew something was seriously wrong." Martin was by then safely under arrest on the navy ship.

It was now Saturday morning.

> I was awakened at half past five by loud banging. The Special Branch were outside in numbers. They came in and the first thing they said to me was, "Where's Martin?"
>
> "I don't know," I said.
>
> "You do know where he is."
>
> "I don't know where he is."
>
> Then they went searching. They didn't do a raid; they just looked in the house to see who was here, and, of course, there were only the children in bed, and they left. I knew something was very seriously wrong at that stage. What I didn't know was that they knew they had Martin, courtesy of O'Callaghan.

The first she heard of his capture was on the early radio news. "I turned on the radio for the morning news at seven o'clock. There was news that a vessel had been intercepted and was being escorted into Cobh by the navy. In my heart I knew. *God, that's what it's all about.*"

At half past seven or thereabouts, three people arrived into the kitchen. It was the ever-loyal James Sheehan, Patchín McCarthy, brother of Johnny McCarthy, and Sean O'Callaghan.

> I looked at James. "What's happening?" I pleaded.
>
> James told me he didn't know, but that a boat had been intercepted and Martin might have been on it. He didn't say he was for certain but that he might have been on it.
>
> So, I said to him, "Well, what can I do?"
>
> James replied, "I don't know. I don't know what you can do, Marie."
>
> So they left and, as it happened, they were stopped by the gardaí at a road block down the road and arrested. I knew nothing all day. I had people calling to the house, but I could say nothing for certain. But in my heart and soul, I knew it was Martin on the boat.

While Martin was being transferred via Cobh to Cork for interrogation, Marie was trying to cope with protecting her young family while still not knowing for sure where Martin was and how he was.

> I went into the Sinn Féin office in Tralee to see if anybody there knew anything or could do anything. The sense of uselessness and hopelessness was overpowering. It wasn't until nine o'clock on Saturday night that the RTÉ news showed the first pictures of Martin in handcuffs being escorted off the Irish navy vessel. I knew the seriousness of the situation then, so naturally I broke down. I didn't know what to do, although I did realise I had to get a solicitor. I didn't have a phone in the house, so I went to a neighbour

who had a phone. There was a solicitor in town who we would call whenever Martin was arrested. He said he would go to Cobh. Then I rang the gardaí and they said Martin was being taken to the Bridewell in Cork. So I rang the Bridewell, and I got no satisfaction whatsoever. I then discovered he wasn't even there, and they knew nothing of what I was talking about.

When Marie got back home from the neighbour's house, her home was full.

I couldn't see a wall in my house with concerned friends and neighbours everywhere. They had seen Martin on the news. Within a matter of an hour, my house was crazy with well-meaning people. I knew I was pregnant. I had all these toddlers and babies, and my youngest child Cianán, who was visually impaired, was only fourteen months. So I had a screaming child, our eldest son Eamon knew something bad was going on and he was very upset, and so I had a lot of crying children.

Marie recalls vividly the worst night in her life, although there were many other bad days ahead.

"Someone took the three girls to Martin's mother's house. Eamon stayed here with his baby brother, Cianán. Paudie Lynch, God rest him, and Pádraig O'Brien took me over to Áine Lynch's house in the Spa where I could try to get my head together. It seemed like a total nightmare. But it wasn't."

Someone advised Marie to phone her mother who was in Australia at the time. It might be world news. It was just as well that she contacted her, because her mother phoned back within an hour to say it was on Australian television also.

On Sunday morning at five o'clock, Tucker Kelly drove Marie, Michael McCarthy (a brother of Johnny) and Paudie Lynch to Cork. They arrived so early that there was no place open in which to get a cup of tea. They had no access to the Bridewell at such an early hour. They waited for the restaurant at the railway station to open to get a much needed cup of tea. They then headed for the Bridewell.

It was like a place under siege. It was like nothing I'd ever seen before. The Bridewell was just completely sealed off with armed Irish army soldiers and Special Branch men sporting Uzi sub-machine guns everywhere. There is always something to laugh about in tragedy, and I can remember Mike McCarthy was walking in front of me, and he pushed this guy aside, and he said, "Get that out of my face!" He thought it was a photographer with a camera. Sure it was a Branch man with an Uzi. We thought we were all going to be mown down then and there.

There were huge crowds on the streets and around the Bridewell. They wouldn't allow me in to see Martin. We had to stand out in the street. Then a solicitor arrived and demanded that I should see him. I was eventually allowed into the Bridewell at around 11 a.m., I'd say. You go up a winding staircase in the Bridewell, and on every step there seemed to be a Branch man with a sub-machine gun. That really petrified me.

I got to the room and was shocked when I saw the condition of Martin. There was a Branch man with him. He looked very poorly. He was a chronic asthmatic and obviously had not been receiving his daily medication. And that was when the whole awful scenario dawned on me.

Marie knew at that moment that it would be a long time before she saw him or ever held him close as a husband and wife again. The whole visit took a maximum of seven to ten minutes, and that was it. The next time she could put her arms around him again was 29 September 1987 when the open visits were introduced again in Portlaoise. Máirtín would be three years old before Martin could hold him in his arms for the first time.

Martin remembers that the parting was terrible, because he knew it was going to be for a long time. After Martin was allowed to speak to his wife for that few minutes, he had to get his mind concentrating on his own situation again and what the consequences of his actions on the *Marita Ann* might be. He was thinking of the crew and what could be in store for them. On that Sunday evening, they were taken from Cork to Green Street Court in Dublin.

"I remember when we were coming out of the Bridewell in Cork, and I still can see the crowd of supporters in the streets, all of them wishing us well and shouting support. It was very uplifting."

Martin had plenty of time to think on the long drive to Dublin and then back down to Portlaoise again. He pondered where things had gone wrong. Was there a mole in the camp?

In Green Street Court, they were charged and were then brought down to Portlaoise, reaching the prison at about eleven o'clock on the Sunday night.

> I will never forget going up the stairs to the 2's landing. I heard someone banging at a door and calling my name. I went over to the door and it was Nicky Kehoe. Nicky and I were in jail together in the seventies. Nicky Kehoe did thirty-four days on hunger strike when he was only about seventeen years of age in 1975. I was at the top of the stairs anyway, and I heard Nicky calling me through the slot in his cell door. He called me over for a brief few seconds and wished me well. He gave me a Sunday newspaper through the slot in the cell door. I could see his eyes. 'Twas great to see even that much of a friendly face after, you know what I mean, Green Street and the Bridewell and being strip-searched coming into Portlaoise. There was much sarcasm from screws about me returning to Portlaoise Prison again.

One of the first screws I met said, "You'll be interested to know that Mr Stack is dead." I didn't know Stack was dead, though it had been in the news. I took it as a kind of a dig saying, "Stack's death hasn't changed anything, so look out."

Anyway, I forgot about Stack for the moment. They took us up and we got locked up for the night. The next morning at half past eight the doors opened, so all the lads that I knew were down into the cell to see me and to make sure I was okay. They just couldn't be better. By then we had free association as such. So all the lads were there to meet me on the next morning.

Martin recounts the welcome afforded him by his many old friends in Portlaoise on that first morning back inside:

A great fellow by the name of Gerry Rooney was the IRA OC at that time, and he came down and made sure that we had everything. He arranged visits for us if we needed them. On Monday we were debriefed by Jim Lynagh, who was the IRA intelligence officer in Portlaoise. He was trying to ascertain if we could shed some light on what had happened. The debriefing would have had just the IO and the assistant IO present. They were trying to find out what went wrong. They tried to find out did any one of us speak in the barracks and what we said under interrogation. It was for a person's own integrity as well as for the movement's security. That debriefing took a few days. Out of it then Jim Lynagh helped to prepare the case for us. Jim and I go back a long way anyway. He was an old friend. He was a great person. He was a councillor in Monaghan as well for a while. He was named by Ken Magennis in the House of Commons as a leader in the IRA in the east Tyrone area. The Brits were trying to get him for years. They got him with seven other volunteers at Loughgall, in May 1987. He was a great one.

Marie was in bits as she travelled home from Cork.

It was definitely one of the lowest points I had ever been in so far during my life. Good friends of ours from Limerick, Louise and John Carroll, were here when I got home. All Louise said to me was, "What do you do now?"

"I have a choice: I either go under and destroy my children with me or I stay above it and I rear them to the best of my ability. Because, I know I am going to do it alone."

The way she felt then she wanted to break things. She wanted to hit out. She wanted to break windows. She wanted to scream, shout, roar and cry. But whatever she wanted, she didn't want gratuitous sympathy.

"My life had just been destroyed, and I didn't express my feelings outwardly."

She held it all in and would pay the penalty with health problems shortly afterwards. Although she cried a lot, it was never in front of the children. And so a childhood medical problem was waiting just around the corner to recur at this most inappropriate of times in her life. She had had surgery for bowel obstruction when she was fifteen years old, and half of her bowel had been removed. Now by keeping all of her problems and emotions cooped up within herself, she was nursing a time bomb. Her problems went straight to the physically weakest point and manifested itself again.

"I didn't allow my natural emotions release and so my childhood problem of colitis returned. I didn't want my children to see me cry. I wanted to show them that there was security, that I would be there for them, that I could handle this. But I was so wrong, because they thought I was a cold, hard person. Their daddy was gone and why aren't you crying? They probably thought nothing was a problem to me. And they themselves had huge problems."

Back in Fenit, Churchill and the Spa, the parish was

shattered with the news. With close relationships and family ties there, there were many sad homes that weekend. The McCarthy family were very far reaching. A number of gardaí were included in the wide-spread, highly respected family. Gavin Mortimer's aging grandmother, Katey Lynch, and his aunts and uncles lived in the village of Fenit. None had ever broken a law in their lives. The Brownes were a highly respected, hard-working fishing family who had never crossed the law either. The area was shattered. People had all kinds of reasons as to why they were caught. Admiration and pity were the mixed feelings in the Fenit pubs. Everybody knew there were long prison sentences involved in this.

> Martin was arrested three days before Eamon's eleventh birthday, and Cianán was just fourteen months when his dad was jailed, so they and the three girls were inconsolable. They didn't understand. They just wanted their daddy. I was putting on a hard exterior and overcompensating for Martin's loss by my harsh regime of discipline on the kids.
>
> All I remember is sitting at the kitchen table and telling them that a lot of people are going to say an awful lot of things about their daddy. They were not to answer back, they were not to give cheek, they were not to listen and that I was telling them, as their mother, that they must walk out their front gate and always hold their heads very high and be very, very proud of their daddy. They asked why did daddy do it, and I explained to them as best I could to their age group, about the political situation in our country and why their father felt it necessary to give up his family, to give up a normal life. It was to give them a normal life that he did what he did, and that he was trying to reunite his country, to get back the Six Counties. I explained all that to them, but at the end of the day they were children and they wanted their daddy. And then they wanted to know how long

would their daddy be gone away. So I knew the sentence for this would probably have been fourteen years and then in a child's mind they were adding up how old they would be when he got out, and that was very, very hard. And then we decided, right, we were going to take it day by day and do a roster. We would take every day one day at a time, and every day you have to make your daddy very, very proud of you for what you are doing and never, ever answer back or be cheeky when someone says something bad about your daddy. It was the best I could do at the time.

Two of the girls went through terrible times. I remember my eldest girl, Oonagh; she went down to play with her best friend and came home in floods of tears.

"I'm not allowed to play. Her mammy says my daddy's a murderer."

So I had all that to contend with. I had the second one, Toireasa – two girls used to lie in wait and beat her up after school. Again I wouldn't let them fight back. I don't know whether I was right or wrong, but I wouldn't allow it because I felt that if mine were scrapping literally in the street, people would say, "Oh, what do you expect? Their father's in jail." So I probably became a very strict mother. They were not allowed out in the street. They were allowed out to play, but they were not hanging around streets at night. They had to be in bed at a certain time. I had a very strict routine.

Back in Portlaoise, Martin was contemplating an escape attempt from the court on the day of the bail hearing. Sean O'Callaghan was brought in on the plan. Martin still didn't suspect him as the informer.

"The bail hearing came shortly afterwards. I remember Jerry O'Sullivan and yourself [J.J. Barrett] being up to the court as bailsmen for that hearing."

Jerry, an ex-internee from the forties, was a prominent

businessman in Tralee where he founded a large furniture store, floor covering and boat manufacturing business.

"The case came up first in the Special Criminal Court, I think – then in the High Court on 9 November."

They were refused bail in the Special Criminal Court and then it went to the High Court, and they were refused there as well. There was a strange situation attached to the High Court hearing, because for some undisclosed reason Martin and the others were not even brought up from Portlaoise for the hearing. In retrospect, now many years later, the obvious reason why they were not brought up was because Martin had an escape planned from the High Court. And O'Callaghan knew about it.

> I was to escape by a motorbike, after picking up a revolver left in the gents' toilet. Now in normal circumstances they would bring us up to the court, but they just didn't bring us on that day. The bail was refused anyway. So, it was then really that I knew that something was wrong, very wrong, and that the something was around me. My brother Brian told me months later on a visit to Portlaoise, "All the papers are running around saying that this informer is in America, but," he said, "the fucking man is alongside of you. You're fucking blind. He is alongside of you."
>
> So, I was lying in bed, night after night, and going through everything that went wrong, and a few things did go wrong. But then I would think that so many things went right as well, with the IRA being very, very active in the county. They had done an awful lot of very successful operations, and the suspect was involved in many of them. But then I was pondering the plusses and minuses. Working from a tactical point of view, we had done well, but from an agent's point of view, all of those things were irrelevant. The big one was the *Marita Ann*.

CHAPTER EIGHT

MARTIN GOT THE Book of Evidence and was served with additional evidence by Eric Ryan in the cells of Green Street Court. Martin recalls:

There were seven or eight screws outside the barred gate of the cell. I wouldn't go over to the gate to take it. The next thing one of the screws came in and said, "You must know this fellow – this is Eric Ryan – Inspector Eric Ryan – a good footballer too in his day."

I said, "You don't have to remind me. The first time I ever saw that man was in 1962 in the Cork Athletic Grounds." I said, "I saw him coming off the field and his ear was hanging down. He was crying like a baby." So, Ryan handed me the thing and he walked away. He was furious.

Martin met with barrister Seamus Sorahan, for whom Martin has much admiration. They had become friendly when he represented Martin during the trial for the sinking of the *Ocean Billiard*, Andrew O'Connor's boat. Now he was representing him in the *Marita Ann* case. They prepared for the case as best they could, but the result was a foregone conclusion. They had been caught red-handed on the *Marita Ann*.

The trial began on 29 November 1984 and ran for a total of seven days. Evidence was given that the hold of the *Marita Ann* had been found to contain 160 firearms, including 90 rifles and approximately 71,000 rounds of ammunition. Lieutenant Commander Farrell told the court that on passage to Haulbowline a number of craft had approached and he had ordered some ships to be put between these vessels and the convoy. Because of the *Marita Ann*'s cargo, he was suspicious that an attempt might be made to obstruct the naval vessels.

No one denied that there had been cooperation from outside agencies, British and American, and there were accusations from extreme republicans of quislings doing the dirty work for an imperial power. However, the *Irish Independent* on 17 October carried a report that American security had stated that the initial breakthrough had been made by the Irish, and it was generally believed that Special Branch officers in Cork were the first to get an inkling that something was afoot.

Inspector Ryan, in evidence, said that one of the accused, John Crawley, a former US marine, had travelled from America on another vessel and joined the *Marita Ann* on the night of the arrest. He had been in America since the previous December, when he left Dublin for New York. (John Crawley's evidence refuted this statement by Inspector Ryan.) After the cargo had been transferred to the *Marita Ann*, the *Valhalla* had apparently returned across the Atlantic, and on 19 October was under investigation in Boston. Her owner, fifty-five-year-old Leland Schoen of Ipswich, Massachusetts, said he knew nothing of the alleged smuggling. According to a story in the *Irish Independent*, Schoen believed that the ship had gone on a fishing expedition.[1]

Former Kerry footballer Joe Keohane gave evidence on Martin's behalf. Prominent Fenit fisherman and trade unionist Dan Crowley also gave evidence on his behalf.

"One thing that always comes into my mind is the support I got locally, from people like Jack Godley, Jerry O'Sullivan, Dan Crowley, Pete Lawlor, Jackie Moriarty and J.J. Barrett. You know, people of all political persuasions landed up into the court in Dublin. All of those people in court willing to go bail for us. The local support we got always stayed with me. They were brilliant, brilliant people," Martin recalls.

Martin went into the box and gave an unsworn statement.

> I wish to make a brief unsworn statement in relation to the arms and ammunition taken from aboard the *Marita Ann*. I was contacted and told to procure the use of a fishing boat; with this in mind I approached Michael Browne who was skipper of the *Marita Ann* on Saturday 22 [September]. I told Michael Browne that his boat was requested for use in a forthcoming IRA operation.
>
> He was agreeable and he informed me that he had made prior arrangement with his regular crew, that is Gavin Mortimer and John McCarthy, to take his boat, the *Marita Ann*, to Carrigaholt, County Clare, to carry out general repairs to the hull of the said vessel. He said if he was to change these arrangements it would jeopardise the security of the operation. We agreed that in the interests of security of the operation it would be better to leave the prior arrangements standing. I informed Michael Browne that I, along with somebody else, would come on board the *Marita Ann* in the early hours on Tuesday 25 [September]. By prior arrangement I met with John Crawley in the car park of the Lighthouse Bar in Fenit at approximately 1.30 a.m. on Tuesday 25. We proceeded and boarded the *Marita Ann* at approximately 2 a.m., where I

introduced Michael and John Crawley to each other by first names. Michael informed me his crew were already on board in the bunk. We left Fenit pier at approximately 3 a.m. on Tuesday. Sometime next morning I observed Gavin Mortimer and Johnny McCarthy coming from the galley at the wheelhouse. I left the wheelhouse and I spoke with them. I told them this was an IRA operation and for security reasons they had to be brought along. I also told them they were in no danger. I would like to stress that neither McCarthy nor Mortimer were responsible for the arms and ammunition that were found on board the *Marita Ann*. They were just two innocent civilians who got caught up in an IRA operation under circumstances over which they had no control. It was not our intention then or in the future that the arms and ammunition found aboard the *Marita Ann* were to be used against the security forces of the Free State. Thank you.

The use of the unyielding republican terminology "Free State" to designate the Republic of Ireland meant Ferris was withholding his recognition of the legitimacy of the authorities and the state that was trying him, and which was just about to convict and sentence him.

With his words to the Special Criminal Court, Martin Ferris sealed his fate for the following decade. He took full responsibility for the operation. In the course of the case put by the barristers (Martin Kennedy for Gavin Mortimer, D. McCarthy, SC, for John McCarthy), Judge McMahon made the comment that if it took place in Irish waters, it was an offence. But where was the evidence that it took place in Irish waters? The evidence would suggest that it took place in international waters. So any conspiracy or any cooperation by McCarthy and Mortimer with what was seen to be criminal activity, albeit against their will, or questionably against their will, does not constitute an offence in international waters. Martin Ferris believes that is the reason Gavin Mortimer and Johnny McCarthy received suspended sentences.

The verdict was handed down on 11 December 1984. Martin was expecting fourteen years, which was the maximum. He was expecting that Mike Browne would probably get ten and John Crawley would get ten. As it transpired, the three of them got ten years.

> Even though we were hit for ten years, I remember thinking to myself I was well prepared for it. I thought that wasn't bad, seven and a half you're out. I looked at Marie and she was pregnant with Máirtín. But I had the comfort of knowing that I was also very lucky I was from a very good community like Ardfert, Fenit, Spa, Churchill, Barrow. There wouldn't have been much Sinn Féin support at that time, but still they didn't disown Marie. Instead, people of all persuasions looked after herself and our children. I was there for a full ten years because I got three extra years for the attempted jail break in 1985. That wiped out whatever remission I was going to get. All through that period, I think I was very lucky, even though I had a big family and although the financial circumstances were obviously not good. We were poor when I was going in, and they were obviously worse when I was in jail. But we had enormous relief in the fact that the kids were generally welcomed into the whole community. The Youth Club and Peggy Geary, people of all persuasions, were so brilliant. Our own parish behind in Churchill, the church, the football club. They all helped, and although Marie had a very tough ten years, the community and good friends made things very much easier for her.

Marie's account of those years is a sad one.

> We are blessed with a great family, but the story of their childhood is one of much hardship. However, out

of that hardship grew a great bonding and togetherness. The family ranges in age from thirty-one to twenty. Our eldest son Eamon has excelled in Gaelic football and wore the Kerry jersey in a number of grades. He won All-Ireland Vocational Schools and Sigerson Cup medals. He was my backbone during the bad years. Then there's Oonagh, born 1978, Toireasa 1980, Deirdre 1981, Cianán 1983, and Máirtín on 9 May 1985. I was just pregnant with Máirtín when Martin was captured on the *Marita Ann*.

For the first two years of Martin's sentence, Marie continued to camouflage her feelings. In the following May she gave birth to Martin junior at Tralee Regional Hospital; they named him Máirtín in Gaelic after his dad. Within a year she received a heavy hammer blow when an additional health problem developed.

The lowest point was when I had a lump in my breast. It turned out to be benign, but it was a worrying time. I didn't tell Martin. I refused to tell him until I had gone through the test, the biopsy, and then I would tell him, whichever way it turned out. Unfortunately, he found out in jail, indirectly through another prisoner's wife. I don't know how I coped that time. When you look back you think, *God, I could never go through that again*, but when it's there you manage to get through. That was my loneliest point. Because I had no one. I had the six children and Máirtín was only a baby. I looked at him and thought, *God, I have to get through this thing. God is good. He won't leave these children without their mother in this situation.* The relief was extraordinary when the results were benign. I was on a high then for months.

Trips to see Martin in Portlaoise were very difficult, and both Marie and Martin feel that those visits must have left a certain mark on all of those old enough to remember.

Chapter Eight

Those trips to Portlaoise are still nightmares. This was a terrible journey for all of us. I used to take all of them up there for visits after he was first arrested. I would try to get up every fortnight. Of course, it was very expensive. Then it would be once a month because of the cost. Then I had to stop taking them all because I was pregnant and couldn't manage them. I had five children. Then I had a one-hour visit and that was in a cage, a perspex cage, with no physical contact.

Now Cianán was visually impaired, and that was a further problem. He could hear his father, but because of mesh and the perspex he couldn't see him. So he would get hysterical and he would claw, trying to get to Martin, and of course he couldn't get to him. This was also very distressing for Martin as well as for the child.

Deirdre, who was the youngest girl at the time, was exceptionally close to her father; she would try to climb the wire. She would cry to the screw on duty – the prison officer – begging and pleading and begging and pleading, "Can I go and kiss my daddy?" She would start climbing the wire, and it would upset all of us. It would upset Martin, and he would have to go back to his jail cell without a visit because they would all be screaming. So, in the end Martin refused point blank to see Deirdre and Cianán, until the open visits came in. Because, it was doing damage to Martin and to the two children.

Oonagh, the eldest girl, is the one pictured with her daddy at his mother's funeral. That was the first time he was out in the family since his incarceration. It was for seventy-two hours, and the children were naturally overjoyed. But then he had to go back in again. That was bad too.

A journey to Portlaoise entailed quite a bit of organising. In those days there were very few taxis in

Tralee. You would have to pre-book one to get to Casement Railway Station from Ardfert. Now, I had very good friends, and if they knew I had a visit coming up they would be great and would drive me to the train. So I would be up the night before very late preparing things, and I would bath the kids. Then I would have their best set of clothes in a bag, because going up in the old red rattler train, they would be filthy. So I used to have a change in a type of suitcase. We would take the food for the day as well, because we couldn't afford to eat out. So we would pack all the sandwiches. Sometimes some friend would pick us up for the train station and we would get the half seven train and we would get to Mallow at half nine.

That was the most harrowing part of the whole journey, because I had to cross the bridge with these small children and a pushchair – and I was pregnant too. Eamon had to stand in front and everyone held hands like a rope and the last one holding the pushchair. I would have to carry the pushchair across the bridge, up the stairs, across the bridge, down the bridge and sit on an open platform with small children for three quarters of an hour to wait for the connecting train. I don't know how many times I nearly had a heart attack, because children are children! There were no railings and there were trains passing from time to time. So I never relaxed until I got on that train. Then, it would be the Cork train, so we probably wouldn't have a seat. Martin always tried to arrange my visits for a Friday because I would get my Lone Parent pension on Thursday. So the trains would be very busy every Friday with people going home for the weekend.

Then you would get off at Portlaoise around the half one mark, and again it was across the bridge, down stairs, and then it was a long walk along the main Dublin road. It was difficult walking with all of these small children and a pushchair along such a busy main road. Your heart would stop because the traffic was enormous, and you would have to keep the children in line and keep them all up to you until you walked up to the prison gate. If I only had an afternoon visit, I would sit in Egan's Restaurant and I would get drinks or a bowl of soup and maybe eat our sandwiches with that. The waitress there was very good. She knew the situation and she would allow me to bring in my children and my sandwiches: she would allow us to eat them there inside from the weather. And then I would take the children into the toilet and change them into their clean clothes, one by one. Eamon would be minding the youngest ones.

We would then walk from Egan's up the main Dublin Road and into the prison gates. We would then have the strip-searching. We would all be searched and Cianán was the baby at the time. His nappy would be removed. It was ridiculous because no mother would put a child in jeopardy. We would go through all that for just a one-hour visit.

After the visit we would come back on to that dreadful main Dublin Road again. It would then be late afternoon, and the traffic was just a nightmare. So we would walk down that very narrow footpath again. We would sit in Egan's again as long as we could until the evening meals would be ready, and then we knew you would have to leave. We would sit in the railway station waiting room for about another two hours until the Dublin train came along and picked us up. Of course, we never had a seat because it was the Friday evening train. The students and workers would be coming home. So sometimes I would be able to take luggage off the luggage racks and put the smaller children in the luggage rack. We would stand there usually until sometimes Thurles or Mallow, or even at times Killarney. Then you would get a seat. Usually I had good friends like Áine Lynch or Kevin Mahony or someone to collect me. If not, you would stand in line and wait for a taxi. So you would get home again that night about midnight. So it was hell!

During the period from 1976 to 1982, conditions in Portlaoise Prison had remained pretty much the same, although there were some small improvements. The issues which remained the most contentious and potentially explosive were (1) strip-searching, (2) visits and (3) beatings. They had yet to be addressed, and calm would not return to the prison until they were. The night searches were phased out in 1976.

"Only the most vindictive officers resorted to this form of perverted search," according to Ferris. Much, apparently, depended on the particular assistant chief officer (ACO) in charge of the search. If the prisoner was unlucky enough to have anyone associated with the Heavy Gang, a bad search was almost certain, and beatings featured regularly. Solitary confinement continued to be used regularly as men resisted the strip-searches.

However, the tide was beginning to turn against Governor O'Reilly. Dissension among the prison officers was beginning to surface. Animosity towards prison management was now clearly evident. Prison officers were themselves being damaged by the system. Subtle intimidation of the prison officers by management had been going on for many years, but it was becoming so blatant now that those officers who had turned a blind eye in the past could no longer ignore it.

Dissatisfaction amongst the prison officers with their superiors in Portlaoise was gradually building to a climax. The disapproval and displeasure felt within the ranks of the prison officers manifested itself in public at the POA annual conference in 1984. It centred around the treatment of IRA prisoners in Portlaoise during a general search, which took place on Sunday, 30 October 1983. This particular prison search made media headlines at the time. RTÉ, relying on a Department of Justice press release, reported that six prison officers and two prisoners had been injured during the search. Sinn Féin and the prisoners put the numbers of prisoners injured at eighty, but the media virtually ignored this.

While Irish soldiers were suffering ear damage from artillery and gunfire, and building up compensation claims against the Irish government, prison staff were suffering psychological damage for which there may never be compensation or resolution. The negligence towards prison officers by the Department of Justice, which allowed the brutal Portlaoise regime to operate, has never been challenged in the courts.

Prison Officers' Association Assistant General Secretary Tom Hoare said that staff in Portlaoise had been incited by senior officers to use excessive force against prisoners.[2] Hoare told the delegates: "I accuse the minister of negligence in this area. I accuse the management of Portlaoise Prison of being indifferent to complaints. I would hate to be a prisoner making a complaint."

Many officers continued to accept the bullying of staff, some through fear, others through apathy and more again because they were content with their situation.

Martin Ferris himself was not back in Portlaoise until September 1984, but his recollection of his comrades' account of the terrible day still looms large in his mind. He is still angry that nobody was ever brought to task for the outrage. Some of the main culprits are still at large. But accurate reporting of such incidents was scant and one sided as journalists had little contact with the prison population and depended on Department of Justice press releases for material. In effect, the journalists were being held hostage to fortune.

The initial incident began after the prisoners had been locked up at dinnertime, 12:45 p.m. Officers were ordered to search two cells and strip-search the occupants. Searches during the lock-up or at night were totally unacceptable to the prisoners, and up until then it was a practice long discontinued by the officers. In addition, this search came on a Sunday, and this meant breaking a previous agreement that no cell searches were to be carried out on Sundays. It was the only day in the week the prisoners could get some respite from these searches and relax. There was a standing policy to resist any such searches as a unit, as well as resistance by the individuals subjected to the searches.

The two prisoners being searched, who immediately confronted the officers who entered the cells, fought and struggled as best they could while extra officers entered the fray to subdue them. The arrival of dozens of officers on the landings was an ominous sign. It automatically attracted the attention of the prisoners, who were monitoring their movements, knowing full well something was about to happen. The keys were hardly in the doors of the targeted cells when the word got about that this was happening. The prisoners' response was immediate and deafening. Every prisoner was banging on his door with whatever came to hand. Bed ends, tables and stools were employed to produce a cacophony of sound that shook the prison and was heard in the town. Some of the prisoners almost came through the wooden doors, such was the force and anger with which they walloped them. The officers were unprepared for such a reaction. It had the potential to get seriously out of control. Not having the personnel on hand should the prisoners start coming through the doors, the officers ended the searches and left the cells. Once this became clear to the prisoners the protest ended.

At approximately 2:30 p.m., Governor O'Reilly met with the OC, Francis Lucas Quigley, and the IRA adjutant, Paul "Dingus" Magee. During these talks O'Reilly informed the prisoners' leaders that all the cells would be stripped of their contents as a punishment for banging on the doors. The OC, Quigley, explained the reason for the banging and put the prisoners' case to the governor. He stated that the prisoners did not want a confrontation but could not accept these searches. O'Reilly was asked to ensure that they would not be repeated in future.

If O'Reilly persisted with them, it was pointed out, the prisoners would have no option but to resist them and respond as a unit. Responsibility for the consequences would thus rest with the governor. O'Reilly turned a deaf ear to the prisoners' arguments.

The officers set about removing the contents of the cells. All the furniture – lockers, beds, tables and stools – and the prisoners' personal belongings – clothes, family photographs, letters, books and so on – were thrown out on to the landings and out on to the mesh wire which spanned from one side of the landing to the other. This was highly provocative, and tension was running high as a result. The prisoners exercised restraint, however. The main priority was the welfare of the men themselves and the principle involved. If this was the price exacted for registering their protest at the perverted assaults on defenceless prisoners, then the prisoners were prepared to pay this, and more if needs be.

O'Reilly had already put the prison on a general alert. So by 4:00 p.m. the usual complement of officers was well reinforced. Martin says, "Governor O'Reilly was in an agitated, arrogant and abusive mood." His reasoning was that the prisoners would do as he bid and not what the OC told them or else they would suffer the consequences. As far as O'Reilly was concerned, he was governor of the prison and he could do what he liked, when he liked. He would take on the Provos himself.

By this time every available officer, even those who had been off duty at the time, plus extra gardaí, had been drafted into the prison and were on standby waiting for their orders – all the tell-tale signs that major trouble was on the way. Looking through the spyholes in the doors, the prisoners saw all the evidence they needed. One much-feared officer came in from being off duty. Dressed in civilian clothes, he was seen to be taking charge on the landing. He had obviously given up his time off to direct and participate in the forthcoming search. There were huge numbers of officers and gardaí milling around the ends of each landing.

Martin was told by his colleagues who were there on that 30 October, the horrific autumn Sunday in 1983, "The steely look on their faces and the silent stare told you they were psyching themselves up for a fight. None of them was wearing his tie, a sure sign they were about to enter the cells and search the prisoners."

Martin reasons that, in normal circumstances, the gathering of so many men in such a small area would produce a murmur of incoherent voices, the odd guffaw and burst of laughter. Here it was different. Shuffling feet provided the only sound. The silence was almost deafening for the unarmed and unprotected prisoners in an atmosphere of fear and apprehension of what they knew was to come.

When the mass of officers and gardaí moved on to the landings, there was scarcely enough room for their swelling numbers. Scores of them took up positions at the end of each landing, a reserve force to back up those who would shortly enter the cells. Nobody was in any doubt as to the purpose of the search that was on the way. It was a punitive exercise, no more, no less. Governor O'Reilly obviously wasn't content with removing the contents of the cells. He was about to stamp his authority on those "who had the audacity" to oppose his policy of Sunday and night-time searches. He was going to impress on them who was boss of Portlaoise Prison. Every cell on the republican landings would eventually be entered, and with odds of six to one, and more if required, they systematically strip-searched every prisoner.

From first-hand sources Martin confirmed how bad that October Sunday was to be. "Some of the screws and gardaí who had been drafted into the prison for the search had drink taken. It was a recipe for disaster and indiscipline. It was literally giving a drunken mob licence to go on the rampage."

He said that those who had consumed alcohol were particularly vicious during the rampage perpetrated against the defenceless prisoners. Batons, boots and fists were used liberally. The two prisoners initially searched, and many others also, had to endure two searches as the officers picked out certain prisoners for special treatment.

"Any screws who voiced their objections were themselves bullied and intimidated," Ferris asserts.

One officer came close to choking a prisoner to death, having caught him in a headlock. Only the intervention of an officer who noticed the prisoner was losing consciousness prevented possible loss of life.

"In the aftermath of this prolonged and systematic assault on the prisoners, even the attempt to secure medical attention for the injured prisoners was deliberately frustrated," Ferris believes.

A full forty-eight hours would pass before medical attention was received. Martin is sure that this delay was "obviously designed" to allow bruises to heal and hopefully disappear. In total, thirty-nine men were treated by the prison doctor. As many again, though injured, saw no point in seeking medical attention. Three prisoners were hospitalised.

The prison medical practitioner, a Dr Burke, allegedly refused to log some of the prisoners' complaints or to accede to requests by several prisoners to have their medical records transferred to their family doctors. Three prisoners – Philip Campbell, Kevin Campbell and Dessie Ellis – received fifty-six days in solitary confinement as a result of the search. All three were again stripped and beaten after being moved to the solitary wing.

In their statement after the event, the republican prisoners emphasised that the whole episode of 30 October was engineered and orchestrated by Governor O'Reilly to teach the prisoners a lesson and force them to bend to his will. Pointing to the brutal and systematic nature of the assaults on the prisoners, they called for an independent inquiry into the incident. Responding to questions about the incident in a radio interview, the then minister for justice, Michael Noonan, denied the prisoners' allegations. He went on to make the claim that strip-searches did not take place in Portlaoise Prison. He further claimed to be unaware of the existence of closed wire visits. Is it possible that the minister for justice was unaware or misled about the situation in Portlaoise?

At the Prison Officers Association (POA) conference in May 1984, there was a unanimous call from the Portlaoise branch for an independent inquiry into the incidents that took place in Portlaoise Prison on 30 October 1983.

This call sent shockwaves right through the whole system, from the prison service up through the Justice Department and the government itself. It completely exposed the blatant misinformation that had been emanating from the Justice Department spokespersons. The debate at the POA conference confirmed everything the prisoners had been saying for many years.

Many prison officers who spoke confirmed that prison management orchestrated and manipulated the events of 30 October 1983. Others said that Portlaoise Prison could be compared to a Nazi concentration camp and its worst form of mental torture. One delegate named Larry O'Neill (vice-chairman of Portlaoise Branch POA) told the meeting that, "If Hitler wanted generals today he would find plenty of them in Portlaoise. After the war the Nazis said they were only doing their duty and that is what the management in Portlaoise are saying today."[3]

It was also claimed that most of the beatings were carried out on the instructions of Governor O'Reilly and another officer. Furthermore, they claimed that anyone who was prepared to voice objections to the beatings risked being labelled a Provo lover and consequently would face victimisation by prison management. The POA called for an independent inquiry into the events of 30 October.

An inquiry was conducted by the local gardaí. Many key

witnesses were not called to give evidence. However, for once in the history of Portlaoise Prison, the prisoners and the officers were agreed on the need for changes and for an independent inquiry.

A more conciliatory policy was pursued by government after this hiatus. Officially, economic reasons were given for these subsequent changes, pointing to a need for reductions in staffing in both the prison service and the gardaí at Portlaoise Prison. The new policy adopted was to be called the "humane containment policy".

Instead they would promote an educational programme, something the prisoners had been seeking for years, and adopt a more civilised and liberal attitude towards the prisoners. Negotiation and a good working relationship would replace the baton and the boot. To ensure this policy was implemented, the department had to rein in Governor O'Reilly. Power was taken back from O'Reilly and vested in Department of Justice officials. Any major decisions likely to have consequences and provoke trouble would have to be passed in the department first. The strip-searching was phased out as part of this policy. Strip-searching had been a recipe for tension, trouble and confrontation. In one fell swoop, two of the three major bones of contention and factors contributory to producing conflict in the prison were being addressed. This still left the issue of the inhuman closed visits. They too disappeared from the system shortly afterwards.

On 24 November 1985, Ferris was only eleven months into his ten-year sentence when he was involved in another escape attempt from Portlaoise Prison. It was his second attempted jailbreak in ten years, and on this occasion it was very nearly successful. Eleven prisoners succeeded in breaking out of the prison block, while one, Peter Rogers, kept armed cover on prison guards.

The twelve prisoners included some of the best-known IRA volunteers in Portlaoise. The break was led by Tommy McMahon, convicted of Lord Mountbatten's killing

(Monaghan), Peter Rogers (Belfast), Liam Townsend (Armagh), Eamonn Nolan (Waterford), Sean McGettigan (Monaghan) and Jimmy Gavin (Dublin). All of the above were serving life sentences. The other six were Jim Clarke (Donegal), John Crawley (Kildare), Peter Lynch (Derry), Robert Russell (Belfast), Angelo Fusco (Belfast) and Martin Ferris (Kerry).

They had in their possession a number of keys, guns and explosives. Dressed in mock officers' uniforms, they were able to make their way to the main prison gate. It was a feat in itself to get that far, given the security obstacles that had to be overcome. Along the way, and despite the alarm being raised, they opened fourteen separate locks in perfect sequence with the appropriately designated keys in their possession. At this point, only two gates stood between them and freedom. With a key to the last gate in their possession, there remained only the penultimate gate to be dealt with. Built into one half of the steel gate was a door to allow prison staff entry and exit without opening the huge main double doors. This personnel wicket door had a double lock on it, one on the inside and one on the outside. The prisoners placed explosive charges on three locks which held the huge double doors together. Only two of the locks were successfully blasted. Although the third charge detonated, it jammed the bolt holding both doors together. The prisoners were aware that a timber door leading to a toilet had been replaced with a concrete wall. But with a van marked garda waiting outside to ferry them to freedom, their luck ran out when the newly erected steel door jammed during the explosion. A daring escape attempt was foiled with the prisoners only yards from the main road. So near and yet so far.

The *Irish Press* newspaper on the following day stated:

> The prisoners were fitted out in dark clothing with imitation prison officer uniform buttons. They burst from their cells and ran down the landings towards the reception area.

Rogers, who remained behind, was armed with a revolver and an automatic handgun. Staff were told: "We'll blow your heads off," if they tried to interfere and were ordered to lie on the ground until after the explosion.

While Rogers kept cover the eleven raced to the first gate where they held a gun to the prison officer's head and forced him to open up.

Six other gates were opened with duplicate keys before the eleven arrived at the last gate before getting outside the main prison walls.[4]

Luck ran out for Ferris and the other eleven prisoners when they were unable to blow the final gate.

Fortunately for the prisoners, the power of Governor O'Reilly had been seriously curtailed following the events of 30 October 1983. Nevertheless, he did have some latitude in the immediate aftermath of the escape attempt. With the twelve men on the escape now detained in the segregated area and everyone else accounted for, the governor turned his attention to the republican landings. The following morning all the prisoners were herded out into the yard and the officers went to work removing all the furniture and contents of the cells. It took most of the day for them to search the prison from top to bottom. When the search was completed in the late afternoon, the prisoners were taken in from the yard six at the time and each one directed to a cell on E1 landing. As soon as a prisoner entered the cell, he was followed in by the six officers delegated to carry out the strip-search. That a strip-search would be carried out was a foregone conclusion given that the prisoner was outnumbered six to one; brute force would see to that. For the prisoners, however, it was important to register their protest about the unacceptability of strip-searching. The strip-search never had any security value. Both the officers and the prisoners knew nothing would be found. Governor O'Reilly was getting his pound of flesh in return for the embarrassment of such a well planned and executed jail escape attempt.

Ferris described the scene after the attempted jail break: "With the ten other escapees, we were brought to a segregation area of E1 used for solitary confinement. All of us were forcibly strip-searched. All of us resisted as best we could, and we consequently experienced the brutality associated with strip-searches."

On the following day, Monday, every POW in the prison was locked out in the exercise yard, in extremely inclement weather, without shoes or food for the whole day. A sixty-six-year-old prisoner was subjected to the same treatment. All were taken into the prison one by one and strip-searched again. It was a day of mayhem in the prison.

Martin and the other eleven prisoners who had taken part in the escape attempt were each given three months in solitary confinement. He and five others were later charged with possession of weapons and explosives in the Special Criminal Court in Dublin. They each received three-year sentences to run consecutive with the sentences originally imposed on them. In effect, Ferris had lost any hope of remission on his original ten-year sentence for the *Marita Ann* case. Since the other six prisoners were serving life sentences, they were not charged. It is not possible to add to a life sentence!

The minister for justice in the coalition government of the time, Michael Noonan, said that the Portlaoise escape bid was timed to boost the morale of the Provisional IRA, who had suffered a loss of support to the SDLP following the Anglo-Irish Agreement.[5]

Because the escape was attempted on a Sunday when staffing was lower than usual, major changes of officer ratio to prisoners were made as a result. But the most distasteful outcome for the prisoners and their families was Minister Noonan's banning of family visits to the twelve jailbreakers for Christmas.

On Wednesday, 11 December, the *Irish Press* reported that there was obvious collusion between at least two members of staff and the prisoners at Portlaoise Prison. The escape party had acquired fourteen duplicate keys, extraordinarily, all in precise, consecutive sequence, door by door. They had reached the fourteenth door in approximately twenty seconds. They had two firearms, twenty-seven rounds of ammunition and three pounds of explosives. That the lock on the second last big gate had jammed was probably fortunate, as it avoided a bloody shoot-out with the Irish army, with possibly terrible consequences.

The sophistication of the 1985 attempted breakout puzzled management. The shock for them was in the procurement of fourteen keys in precise sequence. Suspicions fell on a number of prison staff, including management. Were some senior staff under pressure from the IRA? Despite exhaustive enquiries and investigation, the inside connection was never discovered. It had to be somebody in a senior position. A number of officers were transferred for various reasons, but the silence between prisoners and sources has held solid ever since.

In 1986 a debate within Sinn Féin nationally came to a head when there was a walkout by supporters of Ruairí Ó Brádaigh and Dáithí Ó Conaill at the Ard Fheis. Abstentionism from taking up seats in Leinster House had been abandoned, leading to a split on ideological grounds in the movement.

At the time Ferris was completing the second year of his ten-year sentence for the *Marita Ann* gun-running affair. Ferris and the other Kerry political prisoners in Portlaoise were made aware of the forthcoming meeting of the breakaway Sinn Féin wing. There was great concern that Sinn Féin in Kerry was about to split irretrievably once more, as some very well-known and respected republicans seemed intent on following the alternative Republican Sinn Féin course.

Kerry Republican Sinn Féin held a meeting of all members in the county in the Ballygarry House Hotel, Tralee, on Sunday, 23 November 1986. Over fifty people attended, representing eleven cumainn. A Kerry Comhairle Ceanntair was elected: Brendan O'Dowd, chairperson (Cloghane); Margaret J. Doherty, vice-chairperson (Currow); Matt Leen, secretary (Tralee); Maurice Dowling, treasurer (Tralee). In attendance were prominent republicans including Ruairí Ó Brádaigh, former president of Sinn Féin, and Bob Murray of Belfast.

Martin Ferris was about to nail his colours to the mast with a decisive intervention. A statement signed by Ferris and the other seven Kerry prisoners was read to the meeting.

> We wish to clarify any ambiguity that may exist amongst Kerry republicans and republican supporters as to the position of IRA prisoners (Portlaoise Prison) with regard to the recent decision by Sinn Féin to end its policy of abstentionism in future Dáil Elections. As Óglaigh na hÉireann personnel we accept the decision taken by the General Convention of the Irish Republican Army (October 1986) as being absolute. Equally we fully support the democratic decision of Sinn Féin taken at the Ard Fheis (2 November 1986). We pledge our complete loyalty to the aims and objectives of the Republican Movement. We wish also, to make known our position regarding the post Ard Fheis walk-out by a small number of Republicans, and the subsequent formation of a group calling itself Republican Sinn Féin. This breakaway group has no sanction whatsoever to speak or act on our behalf, nor have they any authority to run functions or take up Christmas collections or any other collection, in the name of prisoners, or Prisoners' Dependants. We view their activities, sincere though they may be, as harmful to our just cause. It is our earnest wish that those who joined this breakaway group would reunite with our comrades, strengthening all our resolves and determination in securing the unity of our Country

and freedom for our people. Our commitment to a 32 County Socialist Republic is total.

Signed: Martin Ferris (Ardfert), Paddy Boyle (Tralee), Billy Kelly (Tralee), John O'Sullivan (Listowel), Peter Sugrue (Listowel), Michael Browne (Fenit), Paul Magee (Tralee), Angelo Fusco (Tralee).[6]

Paul Magee and Angelo Fusco were Belfast volunteers, and jail escapers from Crumlin Road Jail, who had set up home in Tralee after having to flee the Six Counties.

By taking this action, Martin Ferris and the other signatories to the statement were unequivocally supporting the Sinn Féin leadership of Gerry Adams, Martin McGuinness, Joe Cahill and the leadership of the IRA.

It was Martin's first major public display of political allegiance within republicanism. His activity and input from behind the high limestone walls of Portlaoise Prison would mark him out as a crucial cog in the conflict resolution machinery of Adams, McGuinness and company for the mid-1990s and beyond, into the twenty-first century. Ferris believes that, "Were it not for the support of the prisoners, a more serious split would have happened."

Sinn Féin were to see good days ahead over the ensuing decade, while the star of O'Reilly's rule in Portlaoise was sinking.

Undoubtedly O'Reilly was in charge during tough times. He had a turbulent and controversial career in the prison service and enjoyed the challenge. The former garda from Mayo survived a bomb attempt on his life. On another occasion, three volunteers were arrested in a farmhouse near Portlaoise on suspicion of intent to kill him. Eamon O'Sullivan, Mick Hayes and Albert Flynn were eventually charged with membership of the IRA and possession of firearms.

Without question, O'Reilly hated the IRA. O'Reilly himself was then to suffer ill health when he should have been looking forward to his retirement. In 1986, while still in his mid-fifties, he developed a brain tumor. At all times dedicated to his duty, he put his position as governor of Portlaoise before his own health. He eventually attended St Luke's Hospital in Dublin for cancer treatment as an out-patient, while simultaneously a patient in Mount Carmel Hospital. However, in December 1986 he was back on duty again in Portlaoise Prison. A Russian-style hat didn't conceal the evidence of the undoubted suffering he had undergone during treatment for his brain cancer. Such was his dedication towards his duty as prison governor that in his last weeks of life he allowed his deputy governors to take Christmas Day off and he himself worked a full shift until 8 p.m. He slipped into a coma a few days after his final Christmas Day in Portlaoise Prison and died in early January 1987. His antipathy towards Provisional IRA sustained him to the end. It can be argued that his brutal regime would cast a dark shadow over the staff and prisoners of Portlaoise Prison for decades to follow. Martin Ferris will certainly never forget his years under O'Reilly's regime.

The governor of Mountjoy Prison, John Lonergan, was requested by the Department of Justice to take over the exceptionally difficult reins of control at Portlaoise Prison. He agreed to undertake the immense task for a two-year stint and assumed control in November 1988. He actually stayed there for three and a half years. The immediate task ahead of him was awesome. The exceptionally poor staff/management relationship needed to be tackled urgently. A meeting of all prison officers was called for the Killeshin Hotel in Portlaoise. Three hundred and thirty out of a possible three hundred and sixty turned out for the meeting. Dozens of unhappy officers stood up and vociferously expressed their great dissatisfaction at the working conditions. Lonergan promised the officers change, and they confirm today that he delivered on many of his promises.

Huge girders stuck in holes to prevent attempted ramming of the main gate were the first items to go. This crude system was designed during Governor O'Reilly's time. It had to be manually lifted and replaced by prison officers each time a vehicle entered or left the prison. The staff had been furious at the system for years but were afraid to speak out. With improvements for staff, a correspondingly more humane attitude developed towards prisoner welfare.

If things were slightly improving inside Portlaoise for Martin and his fellow prisoners, it was a different story for Marie on the outside. Under her circumstances every day was a battle. "I remember two years on, I must have been going through another very bad time. I wrote a letter to Martin and just told him everything that was going wrong."

Before that, in her letters she told him that the children were fine, the tap's not dripping, everything's just perfect, and no, she hadn't any money problems. Then all of a sudden, she wrote a different type of letter. "It must have been a real rocket, because everything I ever felt went into that letter. After I posted it, I thought, *My God, what have I done? He is two years into his sentence and he can do nothing to help me out here. Why did I do that?* It was so very selfish of me. I felt I should not have done that. And it was too late; I had posted the letter and I was dreading and dreading the next letter from him, or the next visit."

Her fears were unnecessary, because instead of being upset, Martin found that letter a great relief and help to him too.

He was delighted, because he said that before he thought that I was a superhuman, iron woman. And all I was doing was trying to protect him; I was trying to protect the children. At the end of the day, the only one that was really suffering was me, because I wasn't being honest and truthful with my emotions. So from then on if the tap was annoying me, dripping, I would write it in a letter. If the lads came in from school and said, "Mam, we want to take up music lessons," I'd say, "Write and ask your father."

185

That way it kept him within the family. It was much better after that.

Martin was officer commanding IRA in Portlaoise when John Lonergan became governor. The new man immediately set about easing the tension between prisoners and staff. He encouraged IRA command in the jail to put forward suggestions for improvements. He asked for a plan which would make life easier for the visiting families and for the prisoners. The written proposal went to the Department of Justice, but Ferris said that no tangible reply came back. Instead there were obvious improvements in a more subtle way. "Gradually one identified an improved atmosphere."

For example, Bishop Comiskey of Ferns requested a twenty-four-hour parole for Peter Rogers to attend the confirmation of his son Eamon in Wexford. Governor Lonergan told the bishop that it was quite impossible as Rogers was serving forty years for the killing of Garda Seamus Quaid. Bishop Comiskey asked if it was possible to perform the confirmation inside Portlaoise Prison. Governor Lonergan saw no problem and acceded to the request. And so the bishop, Rogers' wife Deirdre, a party of witnesses and young Eamon had a memorable ceremony and meal to celebrate the big day. Eamon stated afterwards that it was the first time in his life that he had sat down to a meal with his father. Humanitarianism had made a large stride into the precincts of Portlaoise. More would follow as the relationship between governor, staff and prisoners mellowed. Things would never be the same again.

Reflecting some years later on Portlaoise in those times, John Lonergan, the current governor of Mountjoy Prison in Dublin, said:

> There are two sides to every story, and remember, you were dealing with extremes on both sides and with political pressure to prevent escapes at all costs. But there are basic human standards which must be

observed by state services at all times. The utterly degrading practice of anal searches by lay people would certainly be a serious breach of that standard. It is outrageously wrong to expect prison officers to undertake this task and equally wrong to subject prisoners to it. Anal searches, if thought necessary, should be undertaken by medically qualified people only. To be subjected unnecessarily to anal searches twice a day while in solitary confinement was undoubtedly bordering on torture. Prisoners in Northern Ireland had at least the benefit of a mirror being used by the officers to search prisoners anally while squatting. There was no mirror used in Portlaoise.

He stressed the importance of lack of dialogue in the problems experienced then: "In the absence of dialogue, there is a breakdown in communications. This results in a total lack of trust and understanding in the position of either side."

In 1988, Agnes Ferris became seriously ill. She was in hospital in Cork. Martin applied for parole to visit her but was refused. Luckily she recovered and was eventually strong enough to make further visits to see her son in Portlaoise. However, in January 1989, he received the news no prisoner wants to hear. Governor John Lonergan sent for him, "came around his desk, shook hands", and in the most humane way told him of his mother's death. Lonergan granted him parole for seventy-two hours, and for the first time in five years Martin was at home with Marie and his children and saw his county that he loves so dearly. He spent a cherished three days with Marie and his children. A tender moment between his daughter Oonagh and himself is captured in a picture taken at the burial of his mother in Churchill Cemetery, just yards from her home.

Going back into Portlaoise after being three days with his wife and children was one of the most difficult tasks ever to face Martin during his jail years. However, life in the jail was improving, and sports facilities, reading material and general recreation facilities were getting better. Ferris was absorbed with his organisational work as OC. It was rewarding to see the benefits accruing to families as things improved for visiting. Prisoners could now buy biscuits and tea or coffee from the "tuck shop" for their visitors. It was a huge improvement. Prisoners could hold their children in their arms. They could hug their wife or partner. Gone were the days when wives like Marie would try to explain to their young children why their father was secured behind a wire mesh and plastic barrier where they could not touch him. Visiting times were increased from twenty minutes to at least an hour. This was an enormous improvement.

The IRA command in Portlaoise Prison, including Robert Campbell, Martin and others, met with the Visiting Committee to try improving arrangements and to try breaking down the bitterness that existed between IRA volunteers and the screws. They also met with the renowned economist Dr T.K. Whitaker, who was appointed by the Irish government to evaluate terms of reference for lifers in Portlaoise and to explore an avenue for eventual release. There were no allowances made for temporary release for family deaths for forty-year men, lifers or, extraordinarily, remand prisoners. Peter Rogers, Tommy Eccles, Paddy McPhillips and Brian McShane were all doing forty years at the time.

When, on 12 February 1989, Belfast solicitor Pat Finucane was murdered in front of his wife and children by the UDA, in collusion with the RUC Special Branch and a British agent, his brother Dermot was on remand in Portlaoise. Martin went to his cell to break the news.

The terrible tragedy for the Finucane family provided proof of the success of recommendations in the Whitaker Report. Because of it, a new system had been introduced for remand prisoners. A building named Belade House, in a remote part of the Portlaoise Prison complex, was made suitable for bereaved prisoners to receive their family members in dignity and privacy on such an occasion. Dermot

Finucane was able to mourn the death of his murdered brother in privacy with family members as a result.

One day during a visit in 1990 when Martin and I were able to have a cup of tea and a Club Milk, I foolishly asked exactly just how much time he had left. He passed it off casually with the words "just four years, only four years now". I left Martin thirty minutes later to go back home, but as I walked down the Dublin Road towards Portlaoise Railway Station in the dark and cold winter drizzle, my heart went out to my friend. It makes one wonder nowadays just how Marie managed to bring her six children in all kinds of weather conditions to one of the most unfriendly jails in "civilised" Europe.

Inside Portlaoise Prison the prisoners were gradually becoming aware that contact between the IRA and the British government was taking place. Nothing certain was confirmed, but analysing statements and reading between the lines, it seemed that something was going on behind the scenes.

In the 1990s Martin got a huge boost in life when his son Eamon was beginning to make a name for himself in schools football under the tutorship of Tralee Community College principal Billy Curtin. Eamon also made it on to the Kerry minor football team. On a number of occasions when the Kerry boys reached Croke Park for big matches, Martin was allowed twenty-four hour temporary release. His interest in Eamon's football career was another crutch for Martin during those final years of incarceration.

Back in Ardfert, Marie was still demanding a strict discipline from her kids. She now looks back and thinks she was possibly compensating too much for Martin's unavailability to his children.

> Even Eamon, I can remember it was so funny, I remember Billy Curtin ringing me. They had won an All-Ireland in the VEC college, and Eamon was the youngest on the team. He was seventeen, and Eamon was still not allowed out. And Billy Curtin phoned

me and said, "Marie, look, I will be with them. The teachers will be there. We are having a bit of a celebration in the Mount Brandon Hotel tonight."

"Billy, you know Eamon doesn't drink."

I'd say Billy couldn't be kinder to Eamon, but he must have found it difficult to understand my attitude.

"Can I have your permission to let him out?" he asked.

When I think back now that is embarrassing, you know. And Eamon never ever gave out to me for it. He went along with it. He doesn't drink or smoke. He was never allowed downtown when he was at school. And I remember Bill writing me a note and saying that Eamon was the lad that he could trust to go down with money to the sports store to pick up the football jerseys. And Eamon said, "I can't, sir. My mother doesn't allow me downtown during lunchtime."

So again, he had to write a note saying, "Will you give your son permission? I want Eamon to take the money down and bring back the jerseys."

So when you look back now, I was so strict. But I was afraid, I guess, that people would say, "God, look, she is letting them run riot," or whatever. I was very strict. I don't think it did any harm. I felt I had to be above everyone in respect. I wouldn't ask for anything, or take charity. Like even when it came to communions, the Southern Health Board used to give out money but no, no way. I wrote to my sister in Australia who was a dressmaker, and I remember she got material for my daughter's dress for $5, and you know they all wore it. But, I wasn't going to get charity. I think for Martin's sake, I never wanted him to have a problem with his children. And he never had. He had a hard enough time doing time without freedom and without being with his family, so by God I wasn't going to give him any more problems with children going off the rails or writing in to him, "I haven't got money for this and I want a £200 dress for my daughter for the Communion." To me that stuff all meant nothing.

I can remember the worst thing that I think I did. I can remember a lot of the prisoners' wives ticking up in shops all the year in the toyshop in preparation for these beautiful bikes and music centres and everything else because their daddy wasn't home. And I thought, "No. This is not right. I can't do this. I couldn't put myself into debt like that." I did the reverse. I sat all the lads down, and they all believed in Santa. And I said, "Lads, now daddy's in jail, and so you know that mummies and daddies pay Santa to bring all the presents because there are so many children we have to give some money. And I just, you know, I haven't got the money this year to give Santa a lot for your presents. So you will only be getting one thing each. And I can only afford that much!" I can remember at the time it was £10 for each child. And they did not mind; so long as they got to visit their daddy for Christmas they didn't care. And I remember for years that was all that I ever spent on my children. All I wanted to do was start the New Year without debt, because I had to get through another year without Martin. And I did that.

People were very good you know. A lot of people used to bring loads of tins of sweets and biscuits to the kids. And I was paranoid about teeth. So my kids never had sugar. Never had biscuits or minerals or anything. They just didn't have it. Whether Martin was in jail or not, it would have been that way. And they would see these mountains of tins of biscuits and sweets coming into the house. And they knew I only kept one of each and the rest I used to send in to the orphanage for the children who didn't have any mummy or daddy. My kids have said to me in later years, "Do you know how cruel that was?" But, I

don't know why I did that either. Maybe it was my
paranoia about teeth. But I would keep the one tin of
biscuits and sweets. I know people did it out of the
goodness of their hearts. Again – this is not going to
make up for their daddy being here. I didn't want
them to get into that mindset for life. That you com-
pensate anything material for a person who is away.
Maybe I went overboard.

I know my children are great. They have never
brought any trouble to my door. You know, I'm sure
that they have had a lot of problems, but they are
very well adjusted. Well, Toireasa is following the
path of her father. She is now a member of Kerry
County Council. Eamon would be totally apolitical.
You see the boys, Cianán and Máirtín were not
affected. Cianán was a baby. Máirtín was born after
his father was in jail. To all intents and purposes,
Eamon was their father. I mean even to this day,
Martin will tell them to do something and they will
take it as a joke and maybe laugh at him, but Eamon
would just have to look at them and they would do
what Eamon says. The girls and Eamon were very
affected by the whole trauma of prison.

Looking back now, Marie reflects on those dreadful
times for her and her family:

> I know we had a different situation to any other fam-
> ily in the area. I was very isolated from the northern
> political situation here in Ardfert. It was very unusu-
> al to see a political prisoner's wife and family in a
> place like Ardfert. In the north of Ireland it is differ-
> ent. I remember I did take Eamon up to the north to
> Brian Keenan's family's home because as a young lad
> he was finding it very difficult. I felt he needed to mix
> with children with the same problems, with their
> fathers in jail. I would say this was about eight
> months after Martin was arrested. And I knew he

was finding it very tough, and so I took him up to Belfast. We went walking along New Barnsley, and I said, "This little girl's daddy is dead. He is in Milltown Cemetery. This little boy's daddy is doing life," and so it went with every second house in West Belfast. And Eamon then realised just how lucky he was. You know, he got it in perspective then. In Ardfert we were isolated, very isolated from those with similar situations to ours.

In the nineties, along with improvements in Portlaoise in the educational and sporting spheres, sporting lectures and music were introduced. Big sports names such as GAA men Mick O'Dwyer, John O'Leary and Colm O'Rourke, Eamon Dunphy from soccer, and Christy Moore and Frances Black from the world of music visited. The isolation was gradually being removed. Martin looks back at those times as being busy for him in Portlaoise. The camaraderie between the IRA prisoners was important and kept many a family man going through the down days when one missed the family too much. But Martin's belief in the cause that put him into Portlaoise was his own personal mainstay for all of those years away from Marie and their children.

CHAPTER NINE

O N Saturday, 11 September 1994, Martin Ferris was released from Portlaoise Prison. He was forty-two years old and had completed a full ten years without a single day's remission. He was collected by Kevin O'Mahony and headed straight for Tralee, where he purchased football boots and playing gear before heading for Dingle to play a Gaelic football match in aid of the Tom Moore Children Benefit Fund. Tom Moore had been a great friend of Martin's and they had won Kerry Novice football championship medals together with local club, Churchill, in 1972. A young widower, Tom was drowned off a boat in Dingle and left young children. In that benefit match for Tom's children, Martin lined out with great football names such as Mick O'Connell, Tom Long, Paidí Ó Sé, Mícheál Ó Sé, hurler Frank Cummins and many other stars.

An exceptionally happy and proud Marie and family saw Martin play that football match on his first evening of freedom. The transition for every one of them lay ahead.

Getting used to each other would not be easy. It would be the next big challenge facing the Ferris family.

The first IRA ceasefire had been eleven days old when Martin was released from Portlaoise. He now had a number of choices before him. He could go home and make a life for himself and his family. He could rejoin the IRA. However, he chose to commit himself totally to the Sinn Féin peace strategy. With the peace process now in its infancy, he saw an opportunity where the reasons for conflict could be resolved, through peaceful means. After spending the best part of twenty-five years fighting a war, it was a decision he felt he had to take. He wanted to take another route, a route where no one else would put their life or liberty at stake. He had seen the reality of war. An opportunity now existed, which might not have presented itself again for a long time. So, 11 September 1994 was to be the beginning of Martin's path to peace. And, unbeknownst to him at the time, it was a path that was to lead him to 10 Downing Street and a seat in Leinster House.

A month later, a welcome-home party was held at the Earl of Desmond Hotel, and close to a thousand people attended. Johnny Walker of the Birmingham Six was invited on to the stage to share Martin's big night. The turnout of friends and supporters was a fair indication for the political future of the man who had left the county in September 1984 to serve a decade behind bars for his beliefs. Now he was back, and politics in Kerry were about to change utterly.

After a large part of his lifetime in the service of the IRA, it now seemed only natural that Martin would involve himself in the huge strides being undertaken by Sinn Féin in the political field. Immediately after his release, he was appointed by Sinn Féin Ard Comhairle (High Council) as Sinn Féin delegate to the Forum for Peace and Reconciliation at Dublin Castle.

Although he was constantly declaring his commitment

to the road to peace, the attention of the Kerry gardaí was a continual thorn in his life and that of his family.

Marie sadly recounts one ill-timed visit from the Special Branch on Martin's third Christmas at home for ten years.

On the third Christmas Eve after Martin's release, there was an intensive raid in the morning. In fact, they did a couple of the neighbours as well. The neighbour across the road had children who believed in Santa at the time. The Branch emptied out black garbage sacks containing the Santa parcels. And my next-door neighbour was raided too. In all the years I had never once opened my mouth in a raid. If they asked me for a chair so that they could get in the attic, I would give it to them. I never abused any of them. But it was Christmas Eve – that they would have the audacity to search on that particular day, of all days. I lost it. I just completely lost it. It was early in the morning as well. I had never, ever overreacted. I think it was all the years of pent-up emotion, and I just let fly, and they must have thought, *Martin was very lucky to be away from her for ten years.*

I completely lost it, and I still to this day don't understand why I did it. I hurled abuse. I knew this was not me. They had never seen it before. But they knew they were wrong to search on Christmas Eve. I think they did realise it, because the one that I refused to let through the door sat out in the car. I would not let him through my front door. I said, "You can take over the place, but he will not come through my door."

I remember at one stage running out, screaming, into the street, like a banshee, going to the neighbour, asking if she was okay. I was so gutted that they did go into her home. She is an Australian and not a republican at all. And I came running back into my home, and I noticed that the two Branch men were laughing at me. They were sitting in the squad car.

Which set me off the deep end completely then. And I came charging in to see what they were laughing at, and there I was with a head full of hair curlers! When I think back now – they must have thought I was ready to be put away. This woman screaming, ranting and raving. I looked like Hilda Ogden from *Coronation Street*.

The level of surveillance was almost as bad as in the early eighties. Martin recalls an incident from that era:

I remember a detective pulled up one day in a garda car to question my son Eamon. He was playing around a heap of gravel with Pat O'Driscoll, who later played for Kerry, and his two brothers Timmie and John O'Driscoll. I had been missing for a few days, and the Branch were looking for information about me. The detective called over Eamon and asked him, "Where is your father?" My son said, "I don't know," and the detective got out of the car and slapped him across the face. He asked Eamon again and got the same answer. The detective slapped him across the face again. They kept it from me for a while at home, but I found out. I had two choices. To go and batter the living shite out of him and end up inside in prison, or to go and let his family know what happened. I went to his own house and told his wife what he did to my son.

Ferris could endure considerable disruption himself, but he recalls how difficult it was to watch Marie and his children being subjected to such upheaval. "House raids were ugly. Especially where there are young children in the house. My daughter Toireasa has bad memories of it. She was only three, but she would lock the door of the bedroom she shared with her other two little sisters and keep the gardaí out. Her mother would have to coax her to allow the gardaí in to search the room."

On one particularly heavy raid in or around January

1982, Marie Ferris was strip-searched by a bangharda (female garda), specially brought along with the Special Branch for that purpose.

These searches were very bad. To me they did more damage to the children because they were always carried out in the early morning. I remember Eamon being dragged out of his bed. He was only eight at the time. And a Branch man going through his room with a fine-tooth comb, upending his school bag! And what it did to Eamon at that time was frightening. The girls would be crying. One girl, the eldest girl, Oonagh, was particularly traumatised. She'd find the kitchen door and she would pull the door over and stand behind it, and I would find her after the raid, still standing there trembling. She did that from a very early age; she always did it. She never opened her mouth or made a sound. She just hid behind this door, and she would be very frightened. Then I had Toireasa, who would follow the Branch men from room to room. Where she got her obscenities from I don't know, but she used to let fly, which used to annoy me because I used to think, *They will think that I am putting her up to this*. I had taught all of them, "You don't open your mouth. Hold your head high. They have invaded your home. Do not stoop to their level." But I mean, from two or three she would barricade her wardrobe. She would barricade her room and say they weren't coming in. She then would go out as soon as the Branch would leave, and if the neighbours hadn't seen the raid, she would go knocking on the door and tell the neighbours. You know, that was her way of dealing with it.

Deirdre, again, was very, very young, and to this day she doesn't remember raids. But I remember an extremely bad raid, where I was in the kitchen. Again it was the time O'Callaghan, obviously, tipped them off. He had given Martin something to hide and had told his handler. A bangharda had come as well. It was the first time ever that a bangharda was here. Actually, it was the time of the arrest of Dingus Magee in Tralee in 1982. She was there and about eleven male gardaí. And it was mental; the place was torn apart. And Deirdre was five months old, and I remember them taking her out of her cot and pulling the cot apart. I couldn't understand what a bangharda was doing in my house; never before did it happen. And a detective said to her in the hallway – I was in the kitchen and I was breastfeeding Deirdre at the time – and he said, "Strip-search her."

"You are NOT strip-searching me!" But they did. I didn't realise that I could have objected completely. And it was embarrassing for me because I was breastfeeding, but it was more embarrassing for the bangharda when she searched me in my bra. She had her own comeuppance! I didn't realise until later that I did not have to go through that. But I had nothing to hide anyway. That would have been the worst search – because I was so humiliated. I never, ever forgave those Branch men again. I know one I wouldn't allow through the door again. And you know, they knew that too. Even though they had the power to do it. I would barricade the door and I would say, "He is not coming in!"

During all that time Ferris insists that he never allowed what was happening to his family and himself to become personal.

The gardaí were there and Special Branch were there, and they did all of these things and it hurt an awful lot, but I never allowed it to sidetrack what was the wider picture. The struggle was the wider picture. You could easily lose your focus, very easily. I can't say the same thing for the Special Branch when they

start targeting your family. You must remember
Maurice Prendergast's wife who is a teacher and
James Sheehan's wife who works in the Southern
Health Board. These two women had no involvement, but because of their husbands they were
charged with resisting a search in their house. They
had no hand, act or part in it, but they ended up with
a conviction against them. So, that's how low the
Branch people went in this county. There is an awful
history of it in Kerry. And some of those people are
still in high positions now. They were low level at that
time but are in high positions now.

In autumn 1995, his work at the Forum for Peace and
Reconciliation, which held its first meeting in October
1994, and his work at constituency level in Kerry was
recognised when he was appointed to the Árd Comhairle
of Sinn Féin. Padraig Kennelly, editor of local newspaper
Kerry's Eye, summed up his work over the second half of
the nineties as "keeping a firm grip on the local while
simultaneously cultivating a national image following his
high profile engagement in the peace process".

And although he was engaged in top-level negotiations, he
was still subjected to persistent Special Branch surveillance.

On 29 October 1995 at 12.55 a.m., he was followed
home by two detective gardaí who were stationed at
Tralee. An alleged drug dealer had had his car burned out
in Tralee a few hours earlier. The detectives insisted on
searching Martin's car. He refused, unless they arrested
him first. Immediately outside his home in Ardfert, an
argument ensued as neither side would agree to give way.
The detectives charged Ferris with "intent to provoke a
breach of the peace". Ferris told the gardaí they would be
better employed doing something about the drug problem
in the area. Ferris did not attend the District Court, but
Judge Kelleher sentenced the Sinn Féin man to three
months in jail. Martin appealed the case to the Circuit
Court and it was dismissed.

And so the next few years for Ferris were to follow the same pattern. At every opportunity, the Special Branch tailed him whether in or out of his car. In 1996 he was charged with refusing to allow his car to be searched and for abusive and threatening language. There was on-the-spot reporting by Radio Kerry, and it backfired on those trying to intimidate him, because his support increased as a result, as was clear from the next election result and the vox pop in local radio and comment in the local press. He won the case on appeal to Tralee Circuit Court.

He was on the first delegation in seventy years to meet for official talks with the British, with Secretary of State Mo Mowlam in Stormont on 6 August 1997. For the following years, up to the Good Friday Agreement, he took an active part in many of the talks, especially those involving the prisoners and their future under immunity clauses therein. It was a long way from the continual Special Branch harassment in Kerry to a seat at the table of the British prime minister.

In the Cabinet Room at Number 10 Downing Street, on 11 December 1997, a Sinn Féin delegation met with British government ministers for the first time in seventy-five years. The mood was upbeat. In the three years since Martin Ferris's release from jail, the momentum of the peace process had been building, and now he and his Sinn Féin colleagues stood on the threshold of a breakthrough for all the parties involved in the process. Tony Blair was face to face with some of the most effective Sinn Féin delegates ever to represent Irish republicanism.

Martin Ferris was sitting to the immediate right of Sinn Féin leader and abstentionist Sinn Féin MP Gerry Adams. Sinn Féin's chief negotiator, Martin McGuinness, another abstentionist MP, sat next to Adams on his left. Immediately opposite them were Tony Blair with Mo Mowlam, secretary of state for the north of Ireland , to his right and Paul Murphy, her deputy, to his left, opposite Ferris. The rest of the Irish delegation consisted of the front-line delegates Lucilita Breathnach, Michelle Gildernew, Siobhan O'Hanlon and Richard McAuley.

Nobody at that table had any illusions but that there was much brickwork to be done on the foundations of this bridge of peace between Ireland and Britain, between unionist and nationalist, between Protestant and Catholic, between poor and rich, before the tenuous certainty of the future could be acclaimed for all concerned.

Earlier that day Adams set the tone. On arrival in the hall of Number 10 Downing Street, Downing Street press officer Alistair Campbell greeted Adams and tried to make light conversation with the Sinn Féin leader.

"Well, how are things going with you over there?"

"Did you ever play hurling, Alistair?" asked Adams. "It is the fastest field game in the world. You should try it sometime."

Adams was setting down a marker. There would be no unnecessary small talk from the Sinn Féin group. Down to business now. It was serious work, and the Sinn Féin aim was to control the trend of conversation, even down to the smallest detail, even such as the opener between Campbell and Adams. Nobody was allowed to be sidetracked or any eye to be taken off the ball. Martin Ferris admired his leader's approach: total concentration on what they were in London to achieve.

Casting his mind back to the historic Downing Street meeting, he recalls aspects of the pressures associated with the event.

> You were very much aware of how serious the consequences of the occasion would be in Irish history. Of course, you were a little nervous and apprehensive that we would do the right thing for the people of Ireland. Conscious that the last Sinn Féin delegation, led by Arthur Griffith, with Michael Collins, ignited a terrible civil war. Because of this, you were naturally aware of the significance of the responsibility on your shoulders.

They were engaged in conflict resolution through dialogue and understanding. To get to this point, a great price had been paid by both sides. It was a war. It was a dirty war.

On the walls in these historic rooms hung some of the icons of past British rule. It struck Martin that he was standing in the epicentre from which, for centuries, this once conquering power extended out around the globe.

> The trail of Britain's colonial legacy of chaos throughout the world would have to be impressed on the mind of any reasonably informed student of history who enters Number 10 Downing Street. Just as with our own experience in the north of Ireland, as another sad example. It would make you extremely vexed and exceedingly sad at the capability of the exploitative human being to abuse his power when utter power corrupts and runs riot.

Gerry Adams, at a brief recess, looked up at these pictures and observed to Blair: "It's a strange custom you English have of putting all your failures on the wall."[1]

Ferris mused to himself, *I always thought the Brits put their failures against the wall.*

The Irish delegates were under no illusion regarding the Machiavellian nature of British negotiations. The end always justified the means. The command of realpolitik had outflanked past delegations, not just from Ireland but from the British Empire too. The Sinn Féin delegation was determined not to be outwitted on this occasion.

> You thought of the Falklands, of Derry's Bloody Sunday, of the ignored John Stalker reports, of the hampered Sir John Stevens investigation of British collusion with loyalist gunmen; of Thatcher's sinking of the unfortunate Argentinean cruiser, the *Belgrano*. The 400 young Argentinean sailors deemed irrelevant, and it was sunk well outside the war zone. This didn't seem to matter either, all at the behest of the

British prime minister for political gain. You thought
of the H-Block hunger strikers who gave their lives.
The Brits fought dirty. You thought of Bomber Harris
obliterating German cities with millions of tons of
bombs and fire storms, and how he is still revered by
official Britain today. We all should regret lives lost,
not celebrate them!

The Downing Street meeting was for Martin Ferris a
major milestone. An end to militancy appeared to be on
the horizon, and the beginning of another unexplored journey was dawning, a journey into peace. From now
onwards, the politics of conflict resolution would take priority. However, for this to work, the British government
would have to respect the democratic wishes of the Irish
people and address their brutal legacy in Ireland.

It was also only natural that he would be nominated to
stand for election to local politics. The natural progression
for anybody seeking a seat in Leinster House is via the
local town and county councils. In June 1999, he was elected to Kerry County Council and Tralee Urban District
Council on the same local election day.

Significantly, a new Sinn Féin office was opened in
Tralee in May 2000. Listowel also boasts a similar service
for the people north of the river Feale. Together with his
director of elections, James Sheehan, and a strong team of
young constituency workers, Martin has increased the
number of cumainn (branches) in the North Kerry constituency from two to twelve in the year 2000, and to eighteen currently.

On 7 December 2001, a man was abducted near
Castleisland, County Kerry. Several Kerry Sinn Féin members were arrested, including Martin's director of elections,
James Sheehan. No charges were ever brought against
them.

Again on 11 March 2002, although then a Kerry county councillor and in the middle of a general election campaign, Martin Ferris was driving from Ardfert to Tralee

when he was arrested by gardaí and, for some reason, taken through Tralee another twenty miles to Killarney Garda Station for questioning. He said that he was verbally abused and physically assaulted by one particular garda. Photographs taken after his release clearly show bruising to his chest and abdomen. Some media were aware of Martin's impending arrest before it actually happened. In fact, RTÉ Munster editor Pascal Sheehy contacted the Sinn Féin office in Tralee before Ferris reached Killarney Garda Barracks.

On 19 May 2002, Martin Ferris's political career moved on to a new plane. Heading the poll in his native constituency, he was elected TD for North Kerry, joining four other Sinn Féin TDs in Leinster House. It was exactly thirty-two years since Martin had first joined the IRA. After a turbulent three decades, he was now chosen by the people of his own area to represent them in the highest political chamber in Ireland. And significantly he had been chosen ahead of and had displaced the former tánaiste and leader of the Irish Labour Party, Dick Spring.

By heading the poll with a staggering 9,496 first preference votes – an increase of 3,805 on top of his impressive performance in his maiden general election outing of 1997 – Ferris proved that his hands-on style of politics and closeness to the people was effective and correct.

The general election campaign of 2002 had been a tough one. For Ferris it began late in 2001 when he was subjected to unhealthily close supervision by the gardaí. Wherever the policy of harassment of Ferris had been dreamed up, it was to backfire seriously. The people of North Kerry obviously did not like the constant stream of headlines underpinning the clashes of the gardaí with Ferris.

The voters were well aware that he was instrumental in organising the community to stand up against drug pushers in Kerry. Drugs were a major issue in the election, and for some unknown reason the person doing something about ridding Kerry society of the drug scourge was being constantly harassed by some gardaí. Naturally the national media picked up on the subject, and as a result Ferris was never far off the front pages. The surveillance that had gone on before he was imprisoned was now as intense as ever, although he was totally immersed in the Peace Process.

All through this period Ferris insisted publicly that Kerry had a serious drug problem, and he and his good friend James Sheehan suffered for saying so. But it was later borne out in 2003 by the gardaí themselves. *The Kerryman*, in the summer, had a headline stating "Drug Busts Are on the Up – but so Is the Number of Cocaine Users".

The article stated that Kerry gardaí reported in summer 2003: "Thirty-three drug dealers have been arrested and charged by Gardaí in Kerry so far this year in what is hailed as one of the most successful six-month periods in drug detection in several decades. Routine special intelligence operations carried out by Gardaí in Kerry in the first six months of the year have led to 107 detections of drug offences, some involving major drug barons and dealers."[2]

Ferris had fought the official garda line on the Kerry drug problem for years. He insisted it was vastly worse than officially accepted by top gardaí. Together with Sinn Féin and the community, he confronted drug barons and dealers personally, stretching the rule of law, but gathering massive popular support. Many of the dealers left town.

As the general election campaign of 2002 progressed, it brought a barrage of concerted accusations of vigilantism on to the shoulders of Martin Ferris and Sinn Féin. He and James Sheehan were accused of harassing drug pushers. The election was due in May, and garda surveillance on Ferris and Sheehan was stepped up. Ferris defends vigorously his aggressive attitude towards the drug pushers and drugs bosses.

Now, as an elected TD, the words of Ferris carry added weight. Still, he admits that it is like trying to keep out the tide, that there is much work to be done.

Certainly I tried to counteract the drug pushers. Not alone I myself but the whole Sinn Féin organisation tried very hard to create an awareness of the problem. To bring about a situation where parents and the general community became aware that this massive problem was growing at an incredible pace in our communities. Despite the fact that at that time the chief superintendent said there was no drug problem. And within six months he said there was a drug problem. I have no hesitation in stating that at public meetings in the housing estates, I named the drug pushers openly.

But Ferris insists that he always went to the drug pusher first and asked him to desist from what he was doing. If he didn't desist, then he named him publicly. This happened on two occasions and created a great awareness out there. There were other young people who had been threatened by drug dealers. They would be young drug users themselves who were trying to get off the stuff.

Martin remembers one young fellow who got a bad beating from the drug pusher. He had been supplying for a pusher and then wanted to get out of the racket. The drug dealers were owed some money, and so they beat up the lad who was trying to get out.

"James Sheehan and myself went to his house, and eventually he left Tralee and went to Cork. I didn't advocate or condone vigilantism, but I do understand how it would happen out of frustration. Drugs are destroying lives and whole families, and this must be stopped. Our action and our marches delayed the acceleration of the spread of drugs in the community."

The terrible scenario of the Kerry drug scene had been opening up, and the seriousness of the worsening situation was quite evident to those working on the ground in the communities. And this was not just in working-class communities, but also in all communities in Tralee and throughout north Kerry.

Ferris believes it was running rampant all over the town and all over north Kerry. He had been involved with Partnership and other groups trying to get a situation whereby it became a community issue. He acknowledges that gardaí have a major role to play in it. But, he asserts, so have the community, so have the elected representatives, so has the educational system a role to play in it. It has to be a collective effort. The communities have to be involved.

"They are the best people to police their own community, identifying those who are hooked and so forth. We always differentiate between the user and the pusher. Now there were some people who were pushers, and some who were users and pushers, and we could understand their vulnerability. We don't necessarily condone it, but we try to help them. We got people who were hooked on drugs into institutions where they were helped."

He is happy to state that to this day they have people who are associated with the movement and who were hooked at one time. They are now clean and are involved in helping others who are not so lucky. They were given a chance to rehabilitate, and they are now rehabilitating others. What they did discover when they spoke to people who were heavily involved in drugs was that a sense of hopelessness had set in, a feeling they were nobody and that they felt they were "scum".

"So we felt it necessary to build their self-esteem back up again. We found that people who joined the organisation in Sinn Féin and were working with us to rehabilitate people in trouble with drugs found the system a great help to themselves. They got a sense of value and belonging. That is the best way to build their esteem."

On one occasion a drug pusher claimed that he was abducted by people dressed in garda uniforms. He made a statement that Martin Ferris was present, was armed and had threatened him. When the local community moved against drug pushers, the pushers claimed that Sinn Féin was behind them. They accused Martin of intimidation.

"I make no apologies for challenging the activities of drug pushers. I marched on one pusher's house with the community, and he and some of his family, who were also drug pushers, moved out of Tralee. The people from his new address came to Tralee to ask me to intervene, as he was drug pushing again in his new town. The guards eventually got a conviction against this individual."

Ferris emphatically dismisses as pure fiction the accusation, made by political opponents of Sinn Féin, that their members are in the racket of selling drugs themselves.

> That just would not be tolerated in Sinn Féin, and for that matter, the IRA. Drug dealers would never be tolerated in Sinn Féin. Anybody joining the party would be well aware of that. They have to uphold the constitution of the party. The discipline of aims and objectives are crucial to republicanism. From an internal point of view, we promote an ethic of what Irish republicans should be. They should not be involved in drugs or any anti-social activity. In all the years that I have been involved . . . Jesus Christ, I would go to the end of the earth to deal with somebody internally within the movement if they attempted to sell drugs. I have heard of some people who were once involved with republicanism and who drifted into criminality after leaving republicanism. And maybe you might find one or two of them over the years. I know one in particular who is living in Dublin and who is up to his neck in it, but he is out of republicanism since the 1980s. He is a criminal now, and he has been a criminal for about twenty years.

Martin questions whether this person was ever a true republican. "If he is prepared to compromise republicanism, then he never had the idealism or true heart for the struggle in the first place."

Political opponents in his own county of Kerry choose at times to focus disparagingly on his approach to tackling drug problems. As an anti-drugs activist, he has spear-headed community awareness for a crackdown on pushers and drug barons. For his activity in this field, he has at times drawn the wrath of some members of the media, political opponents and the gardaí upon himself. He has been arrested and accused of vigilantism. Yet as one community member observed, "Drug pushers left Kerry without packing their bags. Ferris instigated their departure."

Regarding the armed struggle, Ferris still holds that the militant road had to be taken by the IRA. He acknowledges that terrible mistakes were made on both sides and vows to work to ensure that a way forward is found through political means alone. The IRA is committed to this now. He met Nelson Mandela in South Africa in 2002 and in this context is reminded of what the great man's opinion was on the subject of military struggle vis-à-vis South African apartheid and the African National Congress (ANC):

> The killing of civilians was a tragic accident, and I felt a profound horror at the death toll. But disturbed as I was by these casualties, I knew that such accidents were the inevitable consequence of the decision to embark on a military struggle. Human fallibility is always a part of war, and the price of it is always high. It was precisely because we knew that such incidents would occur that our decision to take up arms had been so grave and reluctant.[3]

Martin regards as regrettable that over the thirty-odd years man's inhumanity to man was evident in the many battles perpetrated by all sides concerned. But he remains adamant in his summation that it was just such inhumanity, backed by stubborn arrogance, so deeply embedded in the Orange tradition, contrived and controlled by successive British governments, which set the stage for the last thirty years of war. "Unionist intransigence backed by the arrogant dishonesty of successive British governments produced the predictably powerful and savage backlash from the republican community. But all that is in history now."

Mandela further explained: "The armed struggle was imposed upon the ANC by the violence of the apartheid regime."[4] Ferris insists that the same story applies to the Six Counties. Injustices, inequalities, naked and often violent sectarianism, fostered and controlled by the British involvement in Ireland, demanded an armed response by the Catholic/nationalist community. To do otherwise would have been to accept the terrible wrongs that were being perpetrated. The IRA was the vehicle of that response.

There is no going back to war for Ferris. Peace is fully on his agenda, and he does not want to see any more young Irishmen and women suffering the deprivations of prison nor experiencing the inevitable upheaval a war places on a society. In terms of costs, Ferris paid his dues too. He has spent thirteen years in jail, locked away from his family. He has missed the important years in the lives of his children. He saw his wife Marie struggle through ten years of utter hardship trying to bring up a family of six children on her own. He and they experienced hostility and estrangement from mainstream society. He excuses these people because he feels many in the Twenty-Six Counties were unaware of just how bad things had become for north of Ireland nationalists and Catholics. Ferris has endured the psychological and physical hardship of many months in solitary confinement. He was pulled back from death's door on day 47 of the hunger strike in 1977. And he survived the mental and physical conditions in a prison regime which one prison officer afterwards described as having the nature and brutality of a Nazi concentration camp.

However, Martin prefers to look forward, not back, to emphasise what he sees as a great future for many sections of society on this island of Ireland. He does, however, believe that the improvement of standards for less well-off sections must be prioritised by government policy.

He believes the support of his comrades and family crucially sustained him during his ten years in Portlaoise. "I was lucky. I had been very much involved with the fishing industry and with the GAA. We had a big, big bond of friendship built up with people of all persuasions."

By laying aside the gun in favour of the ballot box, Martin Ferris has taken a road much travelled by great republicans of the past. However, he is also conscious of the mistakes of the past that led to the division of the freedom struggle, with the Civil War in 1922–1923 when the then British government outmanoeuvred and compromised the negotiators of the time. The imposition of partition and its acceptance by the Twenty-Six County establishment was to the detriment of the nationalist people, who were abandoned to live the nightmare of partition. The road ahead must address the outstanding reasons why Irish people had to endure so much suffering. Central to the finality of conflict resolution is the issue of partition. Building a united Ireland with equality will be a fitting tribute to all those who have struggled for freedom down through the centuries and, in particular, over the last century.

Martin sees the role of Sinn Féin in peace building, especially with people from the unionist/Protestant tradition, as essential to a lasting peace. Irrespective of religion, colour or creed, equality and recognition of diversity is a must. Ferris believes the peace process will succeed. He recognises that progress may have seemed slow and tedious since 1994, but on reflection eleven years is a very short space in history. He is satisfied that things have come a long way and that Britain's involvement in Ireland is in its last days.

Since the general election of May 2002, Ferris has been a member of the Leinster House parliament and Sinn Féin spokesman for agriculture, marine and natural resources and sport and tourism, and he is currently a member of the Joint Oireachtas Committee for Agriculture and Food. His daughter, Toireasa, is now one of two Sinn Féin Kerry county councillors. She is the current mayor of Kerry.

Chapter Nine

With many years of service to his country still before him, it is possible that Ferris can also go the complete distance to a place at the cabinet table – but, for him, in a thirty-two county united socialist Republic of Ireland. For that would be his wish and his dedicated life's work's fulfilment.

APPENDIX

PATRICK FLEMING WAS born in Swan, County Laois, approximately ten miles from the town of Portlaoise. An active IRA volunteer, he was arrested in 1917 and sentenced to five years imprisonment for republican activities and detained in Portlaoise Prison. When he became aware of Thomas Ashe's death on hunger strike, on 25 September 1917, Fleming had been ill and was detained in a hospital cell. He formally requested the Prison Board to treat him as a political prisoner. Failure to do so would lead to a protest, he warned. When he hadn't received a reply after ten days, he demanded to be returned to his own cell. As soon as he got there, he refused to wear the prison uniform. His protest had begun.

Fleming, now clad only in a shirt and blanket, refused to do prison work. As a consequence, he was placed in a punishment cell where the blanket was taken from him. In the cold and empty cell, naked except for a shirt, a relapse of his illness soon followed. The prison doctor showed concern and directed that he be provided with adequate bedclothes. These were delivered to his cell. Fleming decided to intensify the protest and went on hunger strike. Many concessions were offered to him, but the authorities refused to concede the right to wear his own clothes. He continued his protest. It was a display of courage and defiance which other prisoners found inspirational, some of whom responded to his example. The authorities threatened to use the cat-o'-nine-tails on him and once more left him naked in his cell. This time his health deteriorated to such an extent that the authorities were forced to release him in November 1917.

Upon release, he immediately reinvolved himself in republican activities and consequently was reimprisoned to serve the outstanding part of his sentence in May 1918. When he arrived back in Portlaoise, he was informed that he would not be recognised as a political prisoner. Fleming viewed this as a matter of principle and declared his resistance to all prison rules. He was again placed naked in his cell from 7 a.m. to 8 p.m. without bed or bedclothes. Every morning the officers forcibly attempted to dress him in prison uniform but without much success. Throughout these ordeals, he was frequently brutalised, but regardless of the personal consequences he continued to resist. In desperation, the authorities put Fleming in iron manacles in an attempt to keep the prison uniform on him. They also used a body belt to strap his arms to his body. He was left like this throughout the entire day, making it necessary for him to eat his food from the floor like an animal.

On occasion, Fleming, in a display of exceptional strength, managed to break out of the iron manacles and the body belt, remove the convict's uniform and tear it to shreds. In retaliation, the authorities placed him in what were known as muffs. These were leather flaps and straps which bound the body and arms so rigidly that it paralysed the muscles and tendons. Somehow, he once managed to break out of these too. A special set of muffs were then placed on him which made it impossible for him to eat. He responded by going on hunger strike. When the republican movement were made aware of this, they ordered him off the hunger strike. He was then placed under medical supervision, and an attempt was made to have him certified insane. It failed. Fleming continued his protest, breaking loose from straitjackets and ripping up convict uniforms whenever the officers had manaqed to get them on him. Sometimes it took up to eight officers to continuously watch and restrain him. His constant battles periodically affected his health, and on many occasions the doctor's intervention almost certainly saved his life.

In the summer of 1918, Shortt, the chief secretary for Ireland, visited Portlaoise Prison. The result of his visit was the construction of a special cell which later became known as "Fleming's cell" or, as it was then known "Shortt's Stronghold". This cell was designed to enable the officers to leave Fleming without a special guard. Located on the ground floor (E1), the cell had the ceiling removed, thereby incorporating the cell directly overhead (E2) into the one cell. To deny Fleming access to broken glass. which he frequently used to cut his way out of the straitjackets, the window of the ground-floor cell was bricked up. The only natural light to the cell was coming from the window of the cell overhead, which was approximately sixteen feet from the floor. A new ceiling sloping at an angle of forty-five degrees from the base of the overhead cell door to the ceiling of the overhead cell was built. It had a light bulb in the centre and a special spy hole to observe Fleming from overhead. From this position it was like looking into a pit.

A special radiator was put into the cell to protect Fleming from the cold, which threatened to make his bad health even worse. This radiator became known as Fleming's piano following Fleming's habit of interfering with it and rendering it unworkable. The officers were continually trying to repair it, but Fleming always found some novel way of disabling it. The authorities resorted to encasing the radiator in a wooden jacket to prevent Fleming from gaining access to it, but this too failed. If there was a way around it, Fleming found it. Finally, in an attempt to frustrate Fleming's efforts, the radiator was encased in concrete. When the special cell was completed, the authorities mistakenly believed their problems were solved.

Fleming spent the first day in this cell tearing bedclothes to shreds and destroying the mattress and bed spring. He even smashed the light bulb with the rubber chamber pot. This rubber pot was intended to prevent Fleming's breaking the light bulbs and glass in the cell windows. When the officers opened the cell door for the first time, however, Fleming tossed all the broken material and torn blankets and uniform out on to the landing. A special concrete bed covered with timber was introduced. He was again placed in a straitjacket and the dreaded muffs. On occasions, he even had his hands handcuffed behind his back. Despite all of these restrictions, he continued to amaze everyone by extricating himself from them. Many a time he had to be shifted to the hospital cell, having become ill due to his exertions. Once recovered and back in the special cell, he resumed his one-man war against the policy of criminalisation. Finally, on 1 January 1919, the British authorities deemed Patrick Fleming entitled to political status. He was transferred to Mountjoy Prison, from where he successfully escaped on 29 March 1919.

This specially constructed cell remained as it was until 1980. It served the same brutal purposes against IRA prisoners in the 1940s and also in the 1970s.

Patrick Fleming found himself imprisoned again in 1923 during the Civil War, this time by former comrades, in Mountjoy Prison. He was in the cell next to Ernie O'Malley. O'Malley, in his book *The Singing Flame*, refers to Fleming's bad health: "During the night he often had heart spasms, his body grew rigid, his speech became incoherent. If anyone would touch him during an attack he would regain control, if not, he would feel as if his heart was slowing."[1] He could lie inert for half the following day as a result. As it was necessary for someone to reach in and touch him physically to help Fleming during these seizures, a small hole was made in the wall between the two cells, and O'Malley had on occasion to do just that. Fleming's heart had been seriously damaged by the excessive exertions he put his body through in defying the Portlaoise Prison regime's efforts to break him. His tremendous strength, courage and indomitable spirit has remained an example and an inspiration to political prisoners.

Fleming had a long career as a republican activist. After the signing of the Treaty on 12 December 1921 and prior to the Civil War, he acted under Michael Collins. Tim Pat Coogan mentions Fleming's involvement in the execution of Sir Henry Wilson in June 1922 in London, in his book on Michael Collins.[2] Apparently Peig Ní Bhraonain, who was one of Collin's couriers, met Fleming, who gave her a letter purporting to be an offer of a job as a waitress in Woburn House, London. In fact it was instructions for Liam Tobin, who met her at Euston Station in London. One week later Sir Henry Wilson was shot dead.

During the Civil War, Fleming was active with the republican forces, his involvement resulting in his imprisonment with Ernie O'Malley in Mountjoy. His nephew, Pádraig Fleming, is currently a Fianna Fáil TD for County Laois.

BIBLIOGRAPHY

Adams, Gerry. *Before the Dawn*. Dingle, Co. Kerry: Brandon, 1996.

———. *Hope and History*. Dingle, Co. Kerry: Brandon, 2003.

Cahill, Joe. *A Life in the IRA*. Dublin: O'Brien Press, 2002.

Coogan, Tim Pat. *The IRA*. London: Pall Mall Press, 1970, and Harper Collins, 1993.

———. *Michael Collins, a Biography*. London: Hutchinson, 1990.

Farrell, Michael. *Northern Ireland: The Orange Free State*. London: Pluto Press, 1980.

Feehan, John M. *Bobby Sands: The Tragedy of Northern Ireland*. Cork: Mercier Press, 1983.

Ferris, Martin. Jail notes from Portlaoise. Unpublished.

Harrington, Niall C. *Kerry Landing*. Dublin: Anvil Books, 1982.

Herlihy, Jim. *The Royal Irish Constabulary*. Dublin: Four Courts Press, 1999.

Loftus, John and McIntyre, Emily. *Valhalla's Wake*. Boston: Atlantic Monthly Press, 1989.

Mac Eoin, Uinseann. *The IRA in the Twilight Years 1923–48*. Dublin: Argenta Publications, 1997.

——. *The Survivors*. Dublin: Argenta Publications, 1980.

MacGinty, Tom. *The Irish Navy*. Tralee: The Kerryman, 1995.

Major, John. *The Autobiography*. London: HarperCollins, 2000.

Mandela, Nelson. *Long Walk to Freedom*. London: Little Brown, 1994.

O'Callaghan, Sean. *The Informer*. London: Bantam Press, 1998.

O'Mahony, Sean. *Frongoch: University of Revolution*. Dublin: FDR Teoranta, 1987.

O'Malley, Ernie. *The Singing Flame*. Dublin: Anvil Books, 1978.

Sands, Bobby. *Skylark Sing Your Lonely Song*. Dublin: Mercier Press, 1982.

Sinnerton, Henry. *David Ervine: Uncharted Waters*. Dingle, Co. Kerry: Brandon, 2002.

Smith, Raymond. *The Sunday Independent Complete Handbook of Gaelic Games*. Dublin: Sporting Book Publishers, 1988.

Wallace, Martin. *Drums and Guns: Revolution in Ulster*. London: Geoffrey Chapman, 1970.

Whittemore, L.H. *The Man Who Ran the Subways*. New York, Chicago and San Francisco: Holt, Rinehart and Winston, 1968.

ENDNOTES

Chapter One

1   Tommy "Tucker" Kelly was a good friend of Martin Ferris throughout his life. On occasions when Ferris was in serious trouble with the law over his political stance, quietly spoken Tucker was at hand to be of assistance. A few years ago, Tommy was tragically drowned in a horrific accident in the Atlantic when the fish factory ship he was on was swamped by a giant freak wave while he was working in an open hold. His body was never found.

Chapter Two

1   Michael Farrell, *Northern Ireland: The Orange Free State.* (London: Pluto Press, 1980), p. 256.

2   Nationwide, up to 1,900 Irishmen were sent to the internment camp in Wales. Those interned from Kerry are as follows: Mortimer O'Connor (Abbeydorney); John Byrne, Tommy McEllistrim, Thomas O'Connor (Ballymacelligott); Denis Daly, Mortimer O'Connell, Thomas O'Donoghue (Cahirciveen); Dan O'Mahony (Castleisland); Dermot Corkery, Thomas Fitzgerald, James Moriarty, Michael Moriarty (Dingle); Henry Spring (Firies); J. O'Callaghan (Kenmare); Dick Fitzgerald, Willie

221

Endnotes

Horgan, Pat O'Shea, M.J. O'Sullivan, Michael Spillane (Killarney); John F. O'Shea (Portmagee); Con Murphy (Rathmore); E.J. Barry, Paddy Cahill, Michael Doyle, Bill Farmer, Dan Healy, P.J. Horgan, John Horan, Michael Knightly, Thomas J. McCarthy, Joseph Melinn, Billy Mullins, M.J. O'Connor, Jack O'Reilly, Tom Slattery, James Wall (Tralee); Tim Ring (Valentia Island). See Sean O'Mahony, *Frongoch: University of Revolution* (Dublin: FDR Teoranta, 1987).

After their release from Frongoch by December 1916, many of these men were to play an active role in the fight for freedom and the War of Independence that followed.

3   The team were Pat Walsh, Jim O'Sullivan, Batt O'Shea, Justin Brosnan, Donal Crowley, E.J. Stack, Jed O'Connor, Pat McCarthy, Pat O'Connor, Tom Moore, Martin Ferris, Jim O'Shea, Tadgh Kenny, J.P. Daly, Brian O'Connor. Subs: Denis Horgan, Dermot Crowley, Paud Kelly, Garry Walsh, Philip O'Sullivan, Brendan Walsh, D. O'Sullivan. Selectors: Liam Cotter, Jim Wrenn, Jimmy Ferris, Barty Carmody, Brendan O'Sullivan.

Chapter Three

1   Interview with Dan Keating.

Chapter Five

1   On 25 March 1983, Chief Prison Officer Brian Stack was shot and seriously wounded; he died approximately eighteen months later.

2   Tim Pat Coogan, *The IRA* (London: Pall Mall Press, 1970, and Harper Collins, 1993), pp. 526–7.

3   Nelson Mandela, *Long Walk to Freedom* (London: Little Brown, 1994), p. 623.

Chapter Six

1   Sean O'Callaghan, *The Informer* (London: Bantam Press, 1998).

Chapter Seven

1   John Loftus and Emily McIntyre, *Valhalla's Wake* (Boston: Atlantic Monthly Press, 1989), p. 1.

Chapter Eight

1   Tom MacGinty, *The Irish Navy* (Tralee: The Kerryman, 1995).

2   *The Irish Times*, 26 May 1984.

3   *Evening Press*, 24 May 1984.

Endnotes

4   *Irish Press*, 25 November 1985.
5   *Ibid.*
6   *Kerry's Eye*, 20-26 November 1986.

Chapter Nine
1   Gerry Adams, *Hope and History* (Dingle, Co. Kerry: Brandon, 2003), p. 332.
2   *The Kerryman*, 28 August 2003.
3   Nelson Mandela, *Long Walk to Freedom* (London: Little Brown, 1994), pp. 617–8.
4   *Ibid.*, p. 618.

Appendix
1   Ernie O'Malley, *The Singing Flame* (Dublin: Anvil Books, 1978).
2   Tim Pat Coogan, *Michael Collins, a Biography* (London: Hutchinson, 1990).

INDEX

224

Index

Index

Index

Index

Index